Basic Bible Doctrine and Principles for New and Young Christians

Studying Scripture According to Scripture

Training the Next Generation
by Serving Our Own Generation

Dr. Ken Matto

ISBN 978-1-0980-0729-4 (paperback)
ISBN 978-1-0980-0730-0 (digital)

Copyright © 2019 by Dr. Ken Matto

All rights reserved. No part of this publication may be reproduced, distributed, or transmitted in any form or by any means, including photocopying, recording, or other electronic or mechanical methods without the prior written permission of the publisher. For permission requests, solicit the publisher via the address below.

Christian Faith Publishing, Inc.
Park Avenue
Meadville, PA 16335
www.christianfaithpublishing.com

All scripture quotations are from the King James Bible, Cambridge Edition of 1900.

Printed in the United States of America

For David, after he had served his own generation
by the will of God, fell on sleep, and was laid
unto his fathers, and saw corruption.

—Acts 13:36

Contents

Below are the twenty-seven subjects you will study:

Preface		7
1)	Jesus Christ	11
2)	God	20
3)	The Holy Spirit	25
4)	Prayer	28
5)	The Bible	40
6)	Bible Study	48
7)	Satan	52
8)	The Church	57
9)	Born Again	61
10)	Angels	64
11)	God's Requirements for Christians	66
12)	Giving with Wisdom	68
13)	Giving: A Dynamic of the Christian Life	78
14)	How to Detect a False Gospel	99
15)	Keys to Finding Your Spiritual Gifts	102
16)	Finding God's Will	119
17)	Man	126

18)	Eternal Damnation	130
19)	Heaven	132
20)	Sin	134
21)	Salvation	143
22)	How Does God View the Believer?	162
23)	Prophecy	184
24)	The Cold Water Principle	219
25)	What Is a Christian?	224
26)	How to Identify False Teachers	226
27)	How to Identify True Teachers	238
28)	Online Christian Ministries to Help Further Your Growth!	248
Final Thoughts		251

Preface

Now that you have become saved, you will need help in your new Christian walk. One of the most important aspects of the Christian life is the study of God's Word. You have taken a very important and wise step in desiring to begin a study of Scripture. What this book offers is a foundational understanding of the Bible which will serve as a springboard to both intermediate and advanced studies.

The Bible states in Psalm 119:105:

> Thy word is a lamp unto my feet, and a light
> unto my path. (Psalm 119:105)

The Bible is like a light on our path. Have you ever taken a walk at night and then turned on the flashlight or lit a lamp to light your path so you will not fall and hurt yourself? We all have, especially at camp when we were younger. The Bible is the same way. It is God's light on our path, and we read and study it so we do not stumble as we walk through life. Here is a very interesting verse:

> I will worship toward thy holy temple, and praise
> thy name for thy lovingkindness and for thy
> truth: for thou hast magnified thy word above all
> thy name. (Psalm 138:2)

God has magnified his Word, that is, he has made it greater, elevated it, or raised it above his own name. That is how important

God's Word is to him. It should be that important to us too. God's word is powerful, and he gave it to us as a guide for our entire life.

Many churches offer classes for new believers, and many times, if it is a denominational church, they will teach the new believers according to their church doctrine. What is severely lacking in Christianity today is a working knowledge of the Bible. The majority of Christians are biblically illiterate, that is, if you ask them a question about the Bible or about something in the Bible, they will be unable to answer or they will answer incorrectly. Just because a person is saved for many years does not mean they have a good understanding of Scripture.

I have personally witnessed this illiteracy firsthand. I knew a Christian who was saved for over forty years, and his Bible of choice was a New Testament he could stick in his pocket. What about brethren who know more about sports than the Bible? How will sports help him or her when they face adversity in their lives? This is why this book is based solely upon the Bible so new believers will start off the proper way by gaining a good knowledge of basic doctrine and teachings that will help form a beneficial foundation of understanding that will aid them as they mature into further studies.

This study is based strictly upon the Bible which is the foundation for all other theological works. Do not become discouraged if there is something in the Bible that you do not understand. Rejoice in what you do understand. The Holy Spirit will open your mind to understand the Scriptures. You may be assured that you will receive true instruction from him. Satan, your adversary, has a strong desire to discourage you from studying the Scriptures. If you become a strong Christian, Satan knows that you will become wise to his schemes, but if you fall away from your studies, he will have a field day with you and will cause you to live a defeated Christian life.

The Lord is pleased with those who make a diligent study of his Word. May I encourage you to complete the studies in this book as you will be doing a large amount of Scripture search to ground you in the Christian life. You will also notice that I did not print out all the verses. This is because I want you to search your Bible and find

PREFACE

them. This will also help you familiarize yourself with the sixty-six books of the Bible.

Here are some statistics of the King James Bible:

1) There are 1,189 chapters
2) There are 31,102 verses
3) There are 773,693 words
4) The system of chapters was introduced in 1238 AD by Hugo de S. Caro
5) The verses were created and added in 1551 by Robert Stephanus.[1]

They were the result of man's work to aid in finding certain teachings much quicker.

You have already taken the first step. This book may also serve as a reference manual to help locate specific verses. You must take time to do these studies, because Satan will give you every excuse why you don't have time to study. If you do not own a Bible, then I suggest you purchase a King James Bible (preferably a black letter only edition).

I heartily recommend the following King James Bibles:

(1) A wide margin Cambridge edition which will allow you to make notes in the margin.
(2) Thompson Chain Reference.
(3) The Defined King James Bible available through The Bible for Today Ministries—www.biblefortoday.org.
(4) The Reformation Heritage Bible—www.heritagebooks.org.

The King James Bible was translated from superior manuscripts compared to those used in such corrupted translations as the New International Version or the English Standard Version and many oth-

---

[1] Please note that only the text is inspired and not the chapter numbers or the verses.

ers. All the modern versions are corrupt. Seek purity from the outset of your Christian walk.

> Whom we preach, warning every man, and teaching every man in all wisdom; that we may present every man perfect in Christ Jesus. (Col. 1:28)

Dr. Ken Matto

Jesus Christ

Jesus Christ is the second person of the Godhead. He is neither second in rank nor position, but he holds a different office than God the Father and God the Holy Spirit. As we progress through this study, we will find many biblical passages which teach plainly that Jesus Christ is God. He did not cease to be God when he came to earth. He is eternal without beginning nor end. As long as Christ will be alive, we will be alive, which means forever.

The name Jesus is the Greek translation of the Hebrew name Joshua and it means "Jehovah is Salvation." The name Christ means "The Anointed One." In Jesus's name, we see his purpose, and that is to be the Anointed One of Jehovah to bring salvation to his people (Matthew 1:21).

Jesus has many reference names and titles which I would like to list at this time. Each name gives insight into the diversity of the ministry of the Lord Jesus Christ and what his relation to the Christian is.

1. Advocate—1 John 2:1
2. Almighty—Revelation 1:8
3. Alpha and Omega—Revelation 1:8; 22:13
4. Author and Finisher of our Faith—Hebrews 12:2
5. Beloved Son—Matthew 12:18
6. Captain of Salvation—Hebrews 2:10
7. Creator—John 1:3
8. Deliverer—Romans 11:26
9. Desire of all Nations—Haggai 2:7

10. Everlasting Father—Isaiah 9:6
11. Good Shepherd—John 10:11
12. Great High Priest—Hebrews 4:14
13. I Am—John 8:58
14. King of Kings—1 Timothy 6:15
15. Lamb of God—John 1:29
16. Lord of Glory—1 Corinthians 2:8
17. Our Passover—1 Corinthians 5:7
18. Prince of Kings—Revelation 1:5
19. Redeemer—Job 19:25
20. Shiloh—Genesis 49:10
21. Son of David—Matthew 1:1
22. Son of Righteousness—Malachi 4:2
23. True Light—John 1:9
24. True Vine—John 15:1
25. The Word—John 1:1
26. Saviour—Titus 2:13

Why Do You Think Christ Has So Many Different Names?

There are many other names for Christ written in both the Old and New Testaments. The above list of twenty-six should whet your appetite to study our Lord more in depth. Let me say that we should have an intimate relationship with Christ, and he is not to be treated only as a subject of study. He is our Lord and Savior and must be treated as such. He is called "Saviour" in thirty-seven places in both the Old and the New Testament. It is important to study the passages and context of the passages carefully. The context is the part of a story or discourse; in this case, other passages of Scripture which surround the passage or phrase in question. For example, if I was studying John 14:25, the context would be those verses before it and after it.

Christ's First Coming Prophesied in the Old Testament

1. By God Himself—Genesis 3:15
2. By Jacob—Genesis 49:10
3. By Moses—Deuteronomy 18:15–16
4. By Isaiah—Isaiah 7:14, 9:6
5. By Jeremiah—Jeremiah 23:5
6. By Ezekiel—Ezekiel 17:22
7. By Daniel—Daniel 2:44
8. By Micah—Micah 5:2
9. By Haggai—Haggai 2:7
10. By Zechariah—Zechariah 3:8
11. By Malachi—Malachi 3:1

Why do you think it is important that Christ's first coming was prophesied in the Old Testament?

Prophecies Concerning His Coming:

1. Death—Isaiah 53:4–10
2. Dominion—1 Peter 3:22
3. Kingdom—Luke 23:42; John 18:36
4. Meekness—Isaiah 53:7
5. Priesthood—Hebrews 2:17, 4:14
6. Prophetic Office—Deuteronomy 18:18
7. Rejection—Isaiah 8:14
8. Resurrection—Psalm 16:10
9. Righteousness—Isaiah 11:5
10. Sufferings—Mark 8:31
11. Triumph over Evil—Psalm 110:1, Hebrews 1:13

Why Did Christ Go to the Cross?

1. To save his people from their sins—Matthew 1:21
2. We were spiritually dead—Ephesians 2:1–5

3. To make us spiritually alive—1 Corinthians 15:22; Romans 6:4
4. God's holiness must be vindicated—Leviticus 11:44; Proverbs 15:9
5. Man is totally depraved—Genesis 6:5–6; Romans 3:10–18
6. God loves his elect—Romans 5:6–10
7. To prepare a place for us—John 14:2
8. Man's righteousness could not meet God's standards (Isaiah 64:6). When Adam and Eve sinned, instead of running to God, they made themselves skins of sewed fig leaves. This is symbolic of man's religion which tries to cover his sin and appease God. In Genesis 3:21, we read that God gave them coverings of animal skin, thus symbolizing the death of Christ to reconcile us back unto God (2 Corinthians 5:18).

This was the first blood sacrifice in the Bible.

The Believer's Benefits Resulting from Calvary

1. Romans 8:1—No judgment for sin.
2. Romans 8:15—The fears of this life are removed.
3. Romans 8:15—We are placed into the family of God.
4. Romans 8:17—Heirs of God (Genesis 15:1).
5. Romans 8:17—Joint—heirs with Christ.
6. Romans 8:17—We will be glorified.
7. Romans 8:23—We will be resurrected never to die again.

How God Views the Believer Because of Calvary from Ephesians 1

Vs. 1—Saints—means "Sacred, morally blameless, set apart.
Vs. 3—All Spiritual Blessings—God's spiritual resources commended to us.
Vs. 4—Holy—Set apart, sanctified.
Vs. 4—Chosen—Called out, handpicked.
Vs. 4—Without Blame—Faultless, blameless, unblemished.

Vs. 5—Adoption—Placing as a son or a daughter.
Vs 6—Accepted—Endue with special honor, to be highly favored.
Vs 7—Redemption—Ransom in full.
Vs 7—Forgiveness—Discharge, setting free, remission, liberty.
Vs 13—Sealed—Sealed up for security and preservation.
There will be further studies on this in another chapter.

Biblical Proofs of the Bodily Resurrection of Christ

1. He had flesh and bones—Luke 24:39–40
2. He ate food—Luke 24:41–43
3. He showed Thomas the marks from his crucifixion—John 20:27
4. He was seen by 500 people at once—1 Corinthians 15:6; Deuteronomy 17:6 states that two or three witnesses were enough to confirm an accusation. Here the Lord confirms his resurrection by 500 witnesses. More than the law requires to confirm any event. What if a person was on trial for shooting someone in front of 500 witnesses? Do you think this person would be found guilty?

The Ascension of Christ

1. It happened on the Mount of Olives—Acts 1:12
2. Christ predicted it—John 6:62
3. It was witnessed by the disciples—Acts 1:9–11

Why Christ Needed to Ascend

1. To send the promise of the Holy Spirit—John 16:7–15; Acts 1:8
2. So he may reign over the church universal—Ephesians 1:18–23
3. To prepare for his return on the last day—Acts 1:11

4. To distribute the spiritual gifts—Ephesians 4:10–14; 1 Corinthians 12:5–14; Romans 12:5–8 (At this point do not be concerned about the spiritual gifts. You will have the opportunity to study them as we progress through these studies. Each Christian has at least one spiritual gift.)

His Present Work as High Priest

The High Priest of Israel was the chief intercessor for the people. He was to offer the atoning sacrifice for the entire congregation on the Great Day of Atonement, and we know this day as Yom Kippur. You may find the ceremony in Leviticus 17. To show the fallibility of the earthly priesthood, the High Priest had to offer up the sacrifice for the atonement of his own sins before he could intercede for the congregation. When it came time for the sacrifice for the people, the offering was laid upon the altar, then the High Priest would place his hands upon the head of the burnt offering (Leviticus 1:4).

This was done so that the High Priest became identified or became one with the substitute for sins. The word *offering* in Leviticus 1:4 carries with it the meaning of "brought near." Christ did not have to make atonement for his sins before he died because he was totally sinless, yet he became sin for us (2 Corinthians 5:21).

1. His sinless birth—Luke 1:35
2. His sinless life—John 8:46; 1 John 3:5

The Priest Represented Man to God by Sacrifices and Intercessions. This is How Christ Represents Us:

1. His atoning blood on our behalf—Hebrews 2:17, 3:1; 1 John 2:1
2. He grants to us on the basis of atonement our spiritual and material goods—John 14:16; Luke 22:31–32
3. He intercedes for the church—Hebrews 9:11–15, 24–28, 10:19–22
4. He understands our weaknesses—Hebrews 2:18, 4:14–15

5. Because of Christ's ministry we are now able to enter the Holy of Holies with confidence—Hebrews 4:6. In other words, we may now come into God's holy presence as his children.

The Deity of Christ

In the New Testament:

1. His self-existence—John 8:58, 10:30, 14:10; Philippians 2:6
2. His eternal existence—John 1:13, 8:58; Colossians 1:16–17; Hebrews 1:8–12, 13:8; Revelation 1:8

In the Old Testament:

1. From David—Psalm 45:6–7
2. From Isaiah—Isaiah 7:14, 9:6
3. From Daniel—Daniel 7:13–14
4. From Micah—Micah 5:2

There are three words that describe the Deity of Christ which we will study from the four gospels. The words are not in the Bible but are a descriptive trio of words for deity.

A. Omnipotent—Having all power.
B. Omniscient—Having perfect knowledge.
C. Omnipresent—The ability to be present everywhere simultaneously, free from the laws of time and space.

Omnipotent

1. Over nature—Mark 4:39
2. Over sin—Matthew 9:6
3. Over death—John 11:43–44
4. Over evil spirits—Mark 5:1–16; Luke 4:35
5. Over sickness—Mark 5:25–29

Omniscient

1. He knew the hearts of the Pharisees—Mark 2:8; Luke 6:8
2. He knew the thoughts of the disciples—John 21:7
3. He knew where Nathaniel was before he spoke with him—John 1:48–49
4. He knew the plan of Judas—John 6:70

Omnipresent

1. Where two or three are gathered—Matthew 18:20
2. He is with each Christian—Matthew 28:20
3. He was on earth and at the same time in heaven—John 3:13 (A Great Mystery)

He Received Worship as God By:

1. Nathaniel—John 1:49
2. Demons—Mark 5:6–7
3. The Angels—Hebrews 1:6
4. The Wise Men—Matthew 2:2, 11
5. A leper—Matthew 8:2
6. The Syro-Phoenician Woman—Matthew 15:25
7. Thomas—John 20:28
8. A Blind Man—John 9:38

Other Traits of Christ:

1. He lives within us—Galatians 2:20
2. He is the image of God—Colossians 1:15–17
3. He is the fullness of the Godhead—Colossians 2:9
4. He is our common confession—1 Timothy 3:16
5. He is the blessed hope—Titus 2:13

The Return of Christ

Are we the terminal generation? There is much Scripture pointing to the fact that we are living in the last of the last days. The return of Christ is very near as the following Scriptures will reveal:

1. 1 John 2:18—This verse teaches us that we are in the last hour, and we know this because there is much opposition to Christianity.
2. Hebrews 1:1–2—The Bible refers to the time from the cross to the present as the last days.
3. 2 Timothy 4:3–5—These Scriptures teach us that we may know that we are in the last days by reason of the false gospels that will invade the church.
4. 2 Timothy 3:1–7—These verses warn us of the increase of evil in the last days.
5. Matthew 24:36–39—These verses show that the sinful conditions which prevailed in Noah's time will be repeated in the last days.
6. James 5:3—This verse shows us that people will be obsessed with money and riches. Wealth will be a major goal in the last days.
7. 2 Peter 3:3–4—The last days will be characterized by people who will doubt the return of Christ.
8. Jude 18—The last days will be characterized by those who will mock Christianity while pursuing their own sinful goals.

Watch therefore, for ye know neither the day
nor the hour wherein the Son of man cometh.
(Matthew 25:13)

God

God is the first person of the Godhead and our heavenly Father. Under his name, God and LORD, he is known to have these characteristics:

1. Holy—Leviticus 20:26; Joshua 24:19
2. Just—Deuteronomy 32:4; Zephaniah 3:5
3. Good—Psalm 25:8, 52:1, 86:5
4. Righteous—Exodus 9:27; Psalm 7:9
5. Truth—Deuteronomy 32:4; Psalm 57:10, 91:4
6. Pure—Job 4:17; Psalm 18:26
7. Jealous—Exodus 20:5; Deuteronomy 29:20
8. Compassionate—Psalm 78:38, 86:15, 111:4
9. Merciful—Exodus 34:6; Deuteronomy 4:31
10. Gracious—Exodus 22:27; Psalm 86:15; Jonah 4:2
11. Longsuffering—Psalm 86:15; Jeremiah 15:15
12. Mighty—Genesis 49:24; Deuteronomy 7:21; Isaiah 1:24
13. Angry—Exodus 4:14; Numbers 22:22; Lamentations 2:1–3
14. Able—Daniel 3:17; 2 Timothy 1:12
15. Terrible—(means to be reverenced, feared) Deuteronomy 7:21; Psalm 66:3, 5
16. Great—Deuteronomy 10:17; Psalm 96:4; Daniel 9:4
17. Faithful—Deuteronomy 7:9
18. Glorious—Exodus 15:11; Psalm 8:1; 76:4
19. Perfect—Job 37:16
20. Excellent—Exodus 15:7; Deuteronomy 33:26; Psalm 8:1
21. Life—Psalm 36:9

22. Wisdom—Job 12:16; Psalm 136:5
23. Strong—Job 9:19; Jeremiah 50:34
24. Majestic—Psalm 21:5, 45:3–4
25. Honorable—Psalm 104:1, 145:5
26. Beautiful—Psalm 27:4
27. Sanctified—Isaiah 5:16
28. Peace—Isaiah 9:6
29. A Consuming Fire—Deuteronomy 4:24; Hebrews 12:29
30. Knowledge—1 Samuel 2:3; Job 36:4
31. Eternal—Deuteronomy 33:27; Psalm 103:17
32. Recompensing—Deuteronomy 32:35; Jeremiah 51:56
33. Kind—1 Samuel 20:14; 2 Samuel 9:3
34. Vengeful—Psalm 94:1; Jeremiah 50:15, 28; Romans 12:19
35. Reverend—Psalm 111:9
36. Powerful—Psalm 29:4
37. Dreadful—Daniel 9:4

The attributes of God are a revelation of his true being.

God Exhibits Elements of a Personality

1. He creates—Genesis 1:1
2. He destroys—Genesis 18:20, 19:24–25
3. He provides—Psalm 104:27–30
4. He promotes—Psalm 75:6–7
5. He cares—1 Peter 5:6–7
6. He hates—Psalm 5:5; Proverbs 6:16
7. He grieves—Genesis 6:16
8. He loves—John 3:16
9. He hears—Psalm 94:9–10

Old Testament Passages That Teach the Trinity

1. Genesis 1:1—Elohim; this name is in plural form but it is joined to a singular verb.
2. Genesis 1:26—In the creation of the world.

3. Genesis 3:22—In the expulsion of man from the Garden of Eden.
4. Genesis 11:7—At the confusion of the languages at the Tower of Babel.
5. Isaiah 6:8—Isaiah's commission.

New Testament Passages That Teach the Trinity

1. Matthew 3:16–17—At the baptism of Christ.
2. John 14:16, 26—In the teachings of Christ.
3. Matthew 28:19–20—In the Great Commission.
4. 2 Corinthians 13:14—In Paul's Benediction.

Scriptural Summary

1. The Father is God—John 6:44–46; Romans 1:7; 1 Peter 1:2
2. Jesus Christ is God—Isaiah 9:6; John 1:1; 20:28; 1 Timothy 3:16; Titus 2:13; Hebrews 1:8
3. The Holy Spirit is God—Acts 5:3–4; Hebrews 9:14

Some of the Perfections of God

1. God is self-existent—Exodus 3:13–14
2. God is self-sufficient—Psalm 50:10–12
3. God is eternal—Deuteronomy 33:27; Psalm 102:11–12
4. God has no limitation—1 Kings 8:27
5. God is omnipresent—Psalm 139:7–12
6. God is omnipotent (all powerful)
    A. He rules over his creation—Exodus 14:21–22
    B. Separates light from darkness—Genesis 1:4
    C. Separates waters by the firmaments—Genesis 1:7
    D. Separates seas from dry land—Genesis 1:10
    E. Measures the ocean in his hands—Isaiah 40:12
    F. Weighs mountains in his scale—Isaiah 40:12
    G. Nations are as a drop in the bucket—Isaiah 40:15

H. He looks upon the islands like a speck of dust—Isaiah 40:15
   I. Over men—Daniel 4:30–32
   J. Over angels—Psalm 103:20
   K. Over Satan—Job 1:2; 2:6
   L. Over death—Hebrews 2:14–15

7. God is Omniscient:
   A. God sees all things—Proverbs 15:3; Isaiah 29:15
   B. God knows all—Psalm 147:4; Matthew 10:29–30

8. God knows Mankind:
   A. Our thoughts—Psalm 44:21, 139:2
   B. Our words—Psalm 139:4
   C. Our deeds—Psalm 139:2–3; Revelation 2:2
   D. Our sorrows—Exodus 3:7; Psalm 56:8
   E. Our needs—Matthew 6:32
   F. Our devotion to him—2 Chronicles 16:9
   G. Our weakness—Psalm 103:14
   H. Our foolishness—Psalm 69:5

Other Perfections of God

1. God knows his own—2 Timothy 2:19
2. God knows the end from the beginning—Acts 15:18
3. God is wise—Proverbs 3:19; Jude 25
4. God is immutable—Hebrews 1:10–12
5. God is sovereign—Revelation 4:11
6. God is incomprehensible—Romans 11:33–36
7. God is mysterious—Deuteronomy 29:29; Revelation 10:7
8. God is just—Psalm 103:6: Zephaniah 3:5
9. God is true—John 17:3; Titus 1:1–2
10. God is light—James 1:17; 1 Peter 2:9: 1 John 1:7
11. God is good—Psalm 23:6
12. God is love—Deuteronomy 7:7–8; 1 John 4:8

Describing God by his Names from The Old Testament

1. El Roi—The God who sees—Genesis 16:13
2. Elohim—The Strong one (used in plural)—Genesis 31:29
3. Jehovah—Self-existent one—Genesis 3:14
4. Jehovah Jireh—The Lord will provide—Genesis 22:13–14
5. Jehovah Rapha—The Lord heals—Exodus 15:6
6. Jehovah Shalom—The Lord is peace—Judges 6:24
7. Jehovah Ra-ah—The Lord is my Shepherd—Psalm 23:1
8. Jehovah Tsidkenu—The Lord of righteousness—Jeremiah 23:6
9. Jehovah Shammah—The Lord is there—Ezekiel 48:35
10. Adonai—Lord—Genesis 23:6
11. El Shaddai—The Strong sufficient one who gives—Genesis 49:25
12. El Elyon—The Most High God—Deuteronomy 32:8
13. Jehovah Elohim—LORD God—Genesis 24:7
14. El Olam—The Everlasting God—Genesis 21:33
15. Jehovah Sabaoth—The Lord of Hosts—Psalm 24:10
16. Jehovah Nissi—The LORD my banner—Exodus 17:15

God fills the entire universe, so it is impossible to know everything about him. However, we may gain good insight into his traits, attitudes, and motives by doing a good study in Scripture.

The Holy Spirit

The Holy Spirit is the third person of the Godhead. He indwells the believer (Ephesians 5:18), he is our helper (John 16:7), and he seals us unto the day of our redemption (Ephesians 4:30). The Holy Spirit is never to be referred to as a power or force. The ministry of the Holy Spirit may be summed up as dispensing spiritual gifts to every believer and then helping them to develop the gifts for the building up of the saints and the edifying of the Body of Christ. He illuminates the Scriptures for us to understand.

Traits and Works of the Holy Spirit

1. He intercedes for the praying believer—Romans 8:27
2. He wills who gets what spiritual gifts—1 Corinthians 12:11
3. He searches both the depths of God and the human spirit—1 Corinthians 2:10
4. The Holy Spirit may disallow a ministry in a certain area—Acts 16:6–7
5. The Holy Spirit may allow a ministry in a certain area—Acts 16:10
6. He speaks to Christians through both the Bible and other believers (Beware of those who come to you and say "The Lord told me")—Acts 8:29, 10:19, 13:2
7. Since he is a living being, he is capable of love—Romans 15:30
8. He may be grieved by our sin—Ephesians 4:30
9. He may be quenched—1 Thessalonians 5:19

10. The Holy Spirit is a praying person—Romans 8:26
11. He inspired the Scriptures—2 Timothy 3:16
12. He convicts the world of sin—John 16:8–11
13. He regenerates the believer—John 3:5
14. He sets the believer free—Romans 8:2

Deity of the Holy Spirit

1. He is omnipresent—Psalm 139:7–12
2. He is omniscient—1 Corinthians 2:10–11
3. He is omnipotent—Genesis 1:2; Romans 8:11
4. He is everlasting—Hebrews 9:14
5. He is referred to as God—Acts 5:3–4
6. He is coequal with the Father and the Son:
   A. In Christ's baptismal experience—Matthew 3:16–17
   B. In Christ's temptation—Matthew 4:1
   C. By Paul—2 Corinthians 13:14
   D. By Peter—1 Peter 1:2
   E. By Jesus on the Mount of Olives—Matthew 28:19–20

Names and Titles of the Holy Spirit

1. The Spirit of God—Genesis 1 and 2
2. The Spirit of Christ—1 Peter 1:11
3. The Eternal Spirit—Hebrews 9:14
4. The Spirit of Truth—John 16:13
5. The Spirit of Grace—Zechariah 12:10
6. The Spirit of Glory—1 Peter 4:14
7. The Spirit of Life—Romans 8:2
8. The Spirit of Wisdom, Understanding, Might, Counsel, and Knowledge—Isaiah 11:2
9. The Comforter—John 14:26
10. The Spirit of Promise—Acts 1:4–5
11. The Spirit of Adoption—Romans 8:15
12. The Spirit of Holiness—Romans 1:4
13. The Spirit of Faith—2 Corinthians 4:13

THE HOLY SPIRIT

14. The Spirit of Judgment—Isaiah 4:4
15. The Spirit of the Lord God—Isaiah 61:1
16. The Spirit of Prophecy—Revelation 19:10
17. The Spirit of the Son—Galatians 4:6

The Fruits of the Spirit—Galatians 5:22–23

1. Love—The ability to overlook the sins of others.
2. Joy—The ability to worship God from the heart under adversity.
3. Peace—The ability "to be still and know that I am God" during tough times (Psalm 46:10). According to Romans 5:1, we have peace with God.
4. Longsuffering—The ability to wait on the Lord.
5. Gentleness—The ability to put others before you in kindness and meekness.
6. Goodness—The ability to live by good moral worth, even in private.
7. Faith—The ability to believe God in all situations.
8. Meekness—The ability to be tender in spirit, exhibiting no spiritual pride.
9. Temperance—The ability to rule over the desires of the flesh.

Prayer

1. Praying is seeking and asking God—Matthew 7:7–12
2. Pray according to the Word of God, asking, and receiving—1 John 5:14–15
3. Pray for the knowledge of the unrevealed will of God in a specific situation or need—Colossians 3:1
4. Seeking and finding—Jeremiah 29:12–13
5. Pray for the miraculous intervention of God in your life. I am not speaking signs and wonders, but to handle situations that are out of your control—Matthew 17:14–21

Why Pray?

1. Prayer is imperative—Matthew 26:41
2. Prayer is the only way to request things from God—James 4:2
3. Prayer is joy—John 16:24
4. Prayer can help deliver you out of trouble—Acts 12:1–17
5. Prayer unlocks the treasure chest of God's wisdom—James 1:5
6. Praying is a vehicle for power—Jeremiah 33:3
7. Not praying is a sin—1 Samuel 12:23
8. Salvation is through prayer in faith for those called by God—Romans 10:13
9. Pray without ceasing—1 Thessalonians 5:17
10. Prayer brings hope—Psalm 33:22

PRAYER

How to Pray

1. Christ taught the disciples how to pray (see the exemplary prayer)—Matthew 6:9–13
2. Pray in the name of Christ—John 14:13–14
3. The Holy Spirit interprets when we are short on words and long on problems—Romans 8:26–27
4. Pray that God's will is done in everything—James 4:15
5. Pray for the peace of Jerusalem—Psalm 122:6 (Not for the city in Israel but for the Body of Christ who is the New Jerusalem)—Hebrews 10:22; Revelation 3:12, 21:2
6. Pray for daily necessities—Luke 11:3
7. Pray for forgiveness and forgive others—Matthew 18:21–22
8. Pray in faith—Hebrews 11:6

Hindrances to Prayer

1. Selfishness—James 4:3
2. Unbelief—Hebrews 11:6; James 1:6–7
3. Sin in the heart—Psalm 66:18; Isaiah 59:1–2; John 9:31
4. Husbands who do not honor their wives—1 Peter 3:7

Answers to Prayer

1. Does God answer our prayers?—Jeremiah 33:3; John 15:7
2. Requirements for answers to prayer—Romans 12:1–2; Colossians 3:16–17
3. Delayed—John 11:1–44; Daniel 10:12–14
4. With peace—Philippians 4:6–7
5. With grace—2 Corinthians 12:7–10
6. God answers all prayers, but not always as we ask—Isaiah 55:8
7. Above all, we must endure—Hebrews 10:36

Does God Answer Our Prayers?

God promises in Jeremiah 33:3 that if we call upon him, he *will* answer our prayers. He didn't say maybe or might but that he *will* answer our prayers. We must keep in mind that God may not answer our prayers the way we would like him to. Let me give you four methods by which God answers our prayers. These are the four Ds of answered prayer. It is good that you memorize them so you will be ready when the answers come and you will be able to identify it.

The 4 Ds of answered prayer were given by Dr. Harold Sala back in the 1980s when I was a young believer myself.

Direct Answer

God may choose to answer your prayer in a direct manner. You might pray for something, and God will grant it just the way you asked him for it. This type of answer means you were praying in accordance with the will of God.

Disguised Answer

Let me place before you an analogy which might help you recognize a disguised answer to prayer. You may be praying for your sick child, plus you lack the funds to take him to the doctor, when all of a sudden Uncle Emery from the old country (I am Hungarian) shows up for a visit while you are praying. You immediately view him as another mouth to feed and a cumbersome responsibility at a bad time. Then you start speaking about the sickness your child has. Then Uncle Emery asks you what kind of herbs and spices you have in the house (you are probably thinking to yourself, *What is he going to make? A pot of stuffed cabbage?*) You just "happen" to have the ones he needs.

He starts combining them in a mixture and makes a poultice out of it. He gives it to the child, two days go by, three days go by, and nothing happens; but on the fourth day, the child improves and is sitting up and getting stronger, a week goes by, and the child is cured. You see, God disguised the answer to your prayer in a visit by Uncle Emery. Sometimes our first inclination toward an answer to prayer is that "this can't be the answer to my prayer."

Delayed Answer

Many times, God will answer a prayer, but it will be according to his timing. We may be praying according to his will, but he is engineering special circumstances which will benefit us when it is time to claim the answer. The delayed answer teaches us a lesson in patience and trusting God (Psalm 27:14; Psalm 130:5). Lazarus was dead four days before Jesus raised him from the dead (John 11:39).

Denied Answer

This is the answer we never want to hear, but many times, at a later date, we find out that it was good that God denied my prayer request. When God denies a request, it is being denied by absolute wisdom, plus God knows our entire lives from beginning to end, so it is never to our disadvantage, even though we believe it is.

So we see that no matter when or how we pray, God does answer our prayers, because direct as well as denied is an answer. How many times did you ask your parents for something and they said "no?" It was an answer, but not the one you wanted.

The Exemplary Prayer Commonly Called the Lord's Prayer—Matthew 6:9–13

1. Our Father

The term "our Father" indicates a personal relationship with God the Father, and this only happens when one is saved in the Lord Jesus Christ. The word *our* is a plural word denoting a brotherly relationship with other true Christians. While we can think of God the Father as our own personal Father, he has millions of children worldwide. This is not an implication of the universal fatherhood of God, but it states the universal brotherhood of all true believers. "Father" indicates the familial relationship between God and his children.

2. <u>Which Art in Heaven</u>

God is in heaven, meaning that he is higher than man's earth. "Now know I that the LORD saveth his anointed; he will hear him from his holy heaven with the saving strength of his right hand" (Psalm 20:6). We must realize that God is the king of the universe and heaven and that he is the potter and we are the clay. The fact that we realize God is in heaven means we understand that we are the creation and he is the Creator. We come to God in faith, knowing that we are on earth and he is in heaven.

"But without faith it is impossible to please him: for he that cometh to God must believe that he is, and that he is a rewarder of them that diligently seek him" (Hebrews 11:6). Some of the New Age based religions teach that we can become a god, and that is so false. This is why we acknowledge the fact that the true God is in heaven, and if anyone states they are god, then we know they are false.

3. <u>Hallowed Be Thy Name</u>

God is to be reverenced. Hallowed means to make holy. This is why God's name is never to be attached to a swear word or even some type of "joke." Since Jesus and the Holy Spirit are also God, then their names are not to be used as swear words or even in a common manner. His name is holy, and we find many places in the Bible where it speaks about the worship of God because of his holiness.

David felt this part of prayer was so important that he had a group of men in the temple to do just that.

> Moreover four thousand were porters; and four thousand praised the LORD with the instru-

> ments which I made, said David, to praise therewith. (1 Chronicles 23:5)

> So the number of them, with their brethren that were instructed in the songs of the LORD, even all that were cunning, was two hundred fourscore and eight. (1 Chronicles 25:7)

God is so holy that he is worshipped by special angels.

> And the four beasts had each of them six wings about him; and they were full of eyes within: and they rest not day and night, saying, Holy, holy, holy, Lord God Almighty, which was, and is, and is to come. (Revelation 4:8)

As Christians when we approach God, it must be in the Spirit, that is, we must be saved because otherwise we are in the flesh and God does not hear the prayer of the unbeliever.

> But the hour cometh, and now is, when the true worshippers shall worship the Father in spirit and in truth: for the Father seeketh such to worship him. {24} God is a Spirit: and they that worship him must worship him in spirit and in truth. (John 4:23–24)

Unsaved man is spiritually dead and still in their sins and therefore can never come into God's holy presence.

4. <u>Thy Kingdom Come—Expectation</u>

When Jesus was speaking at this time, there was an expectation that the kingdom of God would arrive when the Messiah came. Many have attached this verse to the false teaching of a literal thousand-year reign of Christ. The kingdom of God which came is made up of those who are born again in the Lord Jesus Christ. The kingdom of God is the eternal church, and it will not be a visible kingdom as some are looking for.

> And when he was demanded of the Pharisees, when the kingdom of God should come, he answered them and said, The kingdom of God cometh not with observation: {21} Neither shall they say, Lo here! or, lo there! for, behold, the kingdom of God is within you. (Luke 17:20–21)

The only time the church is visible is when it is assembled for worship. The ultimate fulfilling of this coming kingdom will be when the new heavens and the new earth are created after this present age is completed with the Great White Throne Judgment, and then God makes everything new for eternity.

5. <u>Thy Will Be Done In Earth As It Is In heaven</u>

At the present time, God's will is that he redeem a people for himself. He did this by establishing his salvation plan on earth. God's will for salvation was established in heaven before the foundation of the world.

> According as he hath chosen us in him before the foundation of the world, that we should be holy and without blame before him in love: (Ephesians 1:4)

Before Adam and Eve sinned, they walked in harmony with God, but once they sinned, that fellowship was broken and had to be restored by means of Christ going to the cross. The ultimate will of God is for his people to become saved. When a person becomes saved in Christ, they are made holy by means of the indwelling of the

Holy Spirit. So the believer is the extension of the holiness found in heaven but on earth.

> For the kingdom of God is not meat and drink; but righteousness, and peace, and joy in the Holy Ghost. (Romans 14:17)

Notice in Ephesians 1:4, we see that the believer should be "holy," and that holiness comes from heaven as God establishes his will that his children will be holy, for he is holy. That holiness comes to the believer by the imputed righteousness of Christ.

6. <u>Give Us This Day Our Daily Bread</u>

Our praying should be as our eating habits—daily. The daily bread that we are to seek is spiritual nourishment. We must seek the face of God in prayer every day.

> Then said they unto him, "Lord, evermore give us this bread." {35} And Jesus said unto them, "I am the bread of life: he that cometh to me shall never hunger; and he that believeth on me shall never thirst." (John 6:34–35)

It is the bread of life that we are to seek. When we ask for daily bread, we are asking for those attributes that the Lord Jesus Christ has to help face our daily trials. We ask for meekness in the presence of trials, we ask for strength to face the day, we ask for wisdom to confront our enemies, we ask for joy to face the losses of the day, and we ask for true love to be able to be a witness to the unbelievers. We may also ask God for daily physical sustenance, but the weightier meaning of this verse is in the spiritual realm.

George Mueller, when he ran his orphanages in England, would always pray for the sustenance needed to take care of the orphans, and God always provided, so it is not wrong to pray and ask God to provide our food for us.

7. <u>And Forgive Us Our Debts</u>

Debt is a word used here to signify sin. We pray that God will forgive our sins, and if you are true believer, then Christ has paid for your sins. Each person is a debtor to God because of our sin, and when we become saved, that debt is paid by the Lord Jesus Christ.

> And forgive us our sins; for we also forgive every one that is indebted to us. And lead us not into temptation; but deliver us from evil. (Luke 11:4)

Luke gives a clear definition that sins are in view.

8. <u>As We Forgive Our Debtors</u>

Do we put forth our hands and say to others I forgive you? One of the best narratives in Scripture which deals with forgiveness is found in Matthew 18:23–35. A master forgave the financial debt of a slave which amounted to 10,000 talents of gold or silver. Each talent weighed fifty-six pounds and eleven ounces. Here is the value of that by today's standards in 4/10/19.

The weight would be 683 ounces. If it was gold, it would be 683 x $1,307.50 = $893,025.50; this equals one talent of gold. 10,000 x 1,102,840.1 = $8,930,255,000. Silver equals $15.19 per ounce. The value would be $103,747,700.

Where would a slave get nine billion dollars or even 103 million dollars? Both of these sums would be absolutely impossible for any slave to raise. Even by today's standards, how many could raise 103 million? What Jesus is showing us here is that no person on earth has the ability to pay for their sins in their entirety. God forgave us our sins because Christ took the penalty of those sins, and as a result, we are totally free from the penalty.

Now within that parable, the one who was forgiven obviously forgot how much he was forgiven and went and found someone who owed him a mere pittance in comparison to what he previously owed. The amount would be approximately eight ounces. A Roman pence was one-eighth of an ounce. If it was eight ounces of silver, the debt would be $143.68, and if it was gold, it would be $10,773.12. What a tremendous difference! 103 million versus 143.68 or 8.93 billion versus 10,773.

When we look at what God has forgiven us for, how could we not forgive someone else who has sinned in such a small way in comparison to our sins? The Lord is basically teaching that those who sin against us will never match the amount and severity of the sins we have committed against God.

> Against thee, thee only, have I sinned, and done this evil in thy sight: that thou mightest be justified when thou speakest, and be clear when thou judgest. (Psalm 51:4)

9. <u>And Lead Us Not into Temptation</u>

The word *temptation* may also be translated "a proving, testing, or trials." In 1 Corinthians 10:13, we read, "There hath no temptation taken you but such as is common to man: but God is faithful, who will not suffer you to be tempted above that ye are able; but will with the temptation also make a way to escape, that ye may be able to bear it."

The word *temptation* in 1 Corinthians 10:13 is the word for "trials." What is the great trial which will come upon the entire world which is common to man? It is Judgment Day, which is the great trial of all people on the earth who are unsaved. If you have become saved, then Christ has stood in your place at your trial, and because of him, you were found not guilty.

What is also in view here is that we pray that God would not allow us to be led into temptation; that is, into a temptation that we may not initially see as a temptation but may see differently.

> And the LORD, he it is that doth go before thee; he will be with thee, he will not fail thee, neither forsake thee: fear not, neither be dismayed. (Deuteronomy 31:8)

We pray that the Lord will go before us and keep us from the path of erroneously engaging something which may be a satanic snare that could lead us away from the path of righteousness. God never leads us into a temptation which could cause us to fall away.

> Let no man say when he is tempted, I am tempted
> of God: for God cannot be tempted with evil,
> neither tempteth he any man: (James 1:13)

We are seeing in this prayer that we pray to be kept from temptations which will cause us to stray, and that is the basic gist of the meaning.

10. <u>But Deliver Us from Evil</u>

Many of the modern versions translate "evil" as "the evil one," which is erroneous. The reality is that Christ already delivered us from the evil one at the moment we became saved.

> Hereafter I will not talk much with you: for the
> prince of this world cometh, and hath nothing in
> me. (John 14:30)

Satan has nothing in the Lord Jesus Christ and has nothing in the believer. Jesus uses this phrase right on the heels of "lead us not into temptation or trials." Those trials which could possibly cause us to stray from the path of righteousness. If I was to paraphrase this section, I would say it this way: "Lead us not into the trial which could cause me to stray from holiness but deliver us from the evil intent and substance of those trials."

We are to pray that we would be delivered from the evil principles of the kingdom of Satan. Even though we have become saved and taken from the kingdom of Satan and adopted into the kingdom of God, we can still be tempted, and if we fall prey to those trials, then we may lose our testimony or something else. We are asking to be delivered from the evil snares that the kingdom of Satan will place before us to try and get us to fall.

11. <u>For Thine Is the Kingdom and the Power and the Glory, Forever, Amen.</u>

This is a great doxology to end a prayer on. A good example would be David's prayer in 1 Chronicles 29:10–19. We are being reminded here that our lives are not our own, because we are in the kingdom of God, and it is his kingdom, and we represent him on this earth at present. Jesus had taught previously "thy kingdom come," and he is speaking about the eternal kingdom of God. We are to recognize that all the power belongs to God because it was through his power that sin and Satan was defeated at the cross, and it was his power that will raise us up on the last day.

We are also reminded that all that God has done for us, from forgiveness to deliverance from Satan, is to the glory of God and not to ours. There are many false preachers out there thinking that they have some type of divine power, and they glorify themselves instead of God. Then Jesus winds up the prayer, reminding us that God's glory, his power, and his kingdom, of which we are a part, will be forever. Then the word *Amen* is used which means "finality, stability, truly, so let it be."

The Bible

The Bible is the Christian's guidebook to a victorious Christian life. It is God's revelation to mankind. To the Christian, it is a book of life. To the unbeliever, it is a book of damnation. The Bible was given to us over a period of 1,100 years. The Old Testament was written between 1447 BC and 445 BC. The New Testament was written between 30 AD and 95 AD. These dates are approximate, but if you round up the time frame, it comes out to about 1,100 years. You will hear that the Bible was written over a period of 1,500 years; this is because they include the 400 years of silence between Malachi and the New Testament. They are just generalizing.

The Bible consists of thirty-nine books in the Old Testament and twenty-seven books in the New Testament. The canon was finalized about 297 AD. The word *canon* means "something set in order." It is applied to the Bible both in the Old and New Testaments.

You may hear some say the Apocrypha books are part of the holy canon, but they are definitely not inspired books and are inferior to the sixty-six which were inspired by God. Normally, you will find these Apocrypha books in Roman Catholic Bibles, and now they are beginning to show up in some of the modern translations which are used by Protestants and Catholics.

My advice is that you do not use any Bible but a King James as you will not find any uninspired book in there. The meaning of the word *Apocrypha* is from the Greek which means "something which is hidden or has hidden meaning." The Bible is God's revealed Word to his children, so the idea of something being hidden from us does not fit with the rest of Scripture; therefore, the apocryphal books are to be rejected. The titles of the apocryphal books are below. Some of the names of the books may be different in various bibles, but they are still not canonical, no matter what name they are under.

1. 1 Esdras
2. 2 Esdras
3. Tobit
4. Judith
5. The Additions to the Book of Esther
6. The Wisdom of Solomon
7. Ecclesiasticus, or the Wisdom of Jesus the Son of Sirach
8. Baruch
9. The Letter of Jeremiah—This particular book is sometimes placed as the last chapter of the book of Baruch. In the book of Jeremiah Baruch was the scribe who wrote the book of Jeremiah.
10. The Prayer of Azariah and the Song of the Three Young Men
11. Susanna
12. Bel and the Dragon
13. The Prayer of Manasseh
14. 1 Maccabees
15. 2 Maccabees

The Bible we have in our King James Version is the Word of God and does not contain the Word of God but *is* the Word of God. This cannot be said about the modern versions. There are none of the original manuscripts existing today. There are some fragments available going back to the first century, but there is no way to tell if they are copies or fragments of the originals. What we have today in the King James Bible is the preserved Word of God.

The earliest New Testament manuscripts available today date back to about 150 AD. It is known as the Syrian Bible or the Peshitta, and it is a translation from the Greek Vulgate which was copied from the original manuscripts. The Peshitta is in approximately 177 manuscripts which are in a British Museum. These two translations are forerunners of the King James Version. So you are on safe ground when you choose the King James Bible.

The Bible you choose will either glorify Christ or it will vilify him as all the modern versions do. Do not fear to use the KJB but refuse to use any other as others will pressure you and come up with all the standard arguments, but you stand firm, and God will bless you.

How God Spoke to People

- Revelation
- Inspiration
- Illumination

Revelation

1. God used angels to deliver messages—Matthew 28:5–7; Luke 1:26
2. Before the Bible was completed, God spoke audibly—Genesis 6:13–21; 1 Samuel 3:1–10; 1 Kings 19:11–12
3. God uses the designed creation to speak to us—Romans 1:20
4. God even used a donkey to bring his message to a disobedient servant—Numbers 22:27–31
5. Before the completion of the Bible God spoke in dreams—Genesis 28:10–17
6. Before the Bible was completed, God spoke in visions—Isaiah 6:1–8
7. God spoke through a Christophany—Judges 6:11—A Christophany was a pre-Bethlehem and post ascension meeting with Christ.

In reference to dreams, voices, and visions, God used these methods up to the time the Bible was completed with the last book being Revelation. There was to be no more new revelation by means of voices, dreams, or visions because we now have the completed

Word of God. God states that no more revelation will be given (Revelation 22:18–19; Proverbs 30:6). This rule applies to tongues or any method people use who believe they are still receiving messages from God. We must be very careful if we believe that we are receiving revelation from God in any form because of the warning in 2 Corinthians 11:14–15 as Satan and his demons are allowed to break the silence barrier.

> And no marvel; for Satan himself is transformed into an angel of light. {15} Therefore it is no great thing if his ministers also be transformed as the ministers of righteousness; whose end shall be according to their works. (2 Corinthians 11:14–15)

Inspiration

The doctrine of inspiration is the correct understanding that all the Word of God was inspired by God. Some unbelievers (even in the church) claim the Bible contains the Word of God and that the inspired words are scattered throughout the Bible. If this is the case, how do you recognize the inspired ones? This would cause tremendous confusion in Christianity, but thanks be to God that he will not allow this to happen to his word. God gives us his assurance that his word is above all the satanically engineered religious books of the phony world religions. When you use your King James Bible, you are using a book that transcends all of man's written words down through the ages.

Scripture Verses on Inspiration

1. Not by human will—2 Peter 1:20–21
2. Fragmented Writings—Hebrews 1:1
3. It is final—John 10:35
4. Spoken beforehand—2 Peter 3:2
5. It is the Word of God—1 Thessalonians 2:13

6. Given directly to men—Jeremiah 36:1–2; Ezekiel 1:3; Acts 1:16
7. Inspiration is given by God—Job 32:8

Illumination

Since there will be no more inspiration, the way which God communicates his spiritual truth to the heart of his children is by the third method of divine communication, which is called illumination. Illumination is the method whereby the Holy Spirit uses to bring divine light to the Scriptures when someone is studying. Illumination allows us to understand the message of Scripture which unsaved man sees as confusing. I have heard illumination described many times in the following manner. "I have read that passage for years, but last night, it jumped out at me like a lion out of a jungle."

When we are praying for guidance, sometimes God will give us the answer by illuminating a Scripture verse, and we will see something in there we never saw before. This is why when we are witnessing to an unbeliever, we cannot expect them to see the same truth which we see. They are viewing it from a fleshly point of view while we see it from God's point of view. The Holy Spirit also uses Christians in his task of illuminating other believers.

1. He used Philip—Acts 8:31
2. He used Paul—Acts 17:2
3. He used Priscilla and Aquila—Acts 18:26
4. He used Apollos—Acts 18:28

The Old Testament refers to itself as the Word of God about 3,800 times. Here are three examples:

1. Amos 3:1
2. Joel 3:1
3. Psalm 119:89

Jesus Endorsed the Old Testament

He referred to:

1. Creation—Mark 10:6
2. Lot's Wife—Luke 17:32
3. Jonah—Matthew 12:40

As you read and study the Scriptures, you will begin to see many quotes from the Old Testament in the New Testament. This is because the Word of God is one cohesive whole and is not to be thought of as two separate halves. The Old and New Testament are deeply enmeshed in each other, which means you can't have one without the other, because they help interpret one another.

There are many churches which teach only the New Testament while rejecting the Old Testament. This is a very erroneous practice, because God has put his approval on the Old Testament by quoting it many times in the New. Both testaments are equally valid and authoritative, because they are both God's Word. To neglect one part is to take away from God's Word, which carries dire consequences. We must never reject any part of Scripture, because it is sin to do so.

This is why I strongly discourage the handing out of New Testaments, only because it is giving only half a Bible and subtly states that the Old Testament is not as important. When I state that the Old Testament is as authoritative as the New Testament, I am in no way suggesting that we are to keep the feasts, which was part of the commandments of God to ancient Israel. All the feasts were symbolic, and in many ways, they looked forward to the coming of the Lord Jesus Christ. We are totally under grace and in no way are we to believe that any keeping of the law in the Old Testament would increase our salvation.

2 Timothy 3:16–17 states:

> All scripture is given by inspiration of God, and is profitable for doctrine, for reproof, for correc-

tion, for instruction in righteousness: {17} That the man of God may be perfect, throughly furnished unto all good works.

All scripture is given by inspiration of God,

The word *inspiration* means God breathed or inspired by God.

and is profitable

Useful for assisting us in having and maintaining a profitable spiritual life while laying down many principles for living in a secular world.

for doctrine,

The systematic teachings of the principles and doctrines laid out in Scripture. To instruct us in God's ways.

for reproof,

For the conviction of our sins, carrying with it the meaning of exposing our sins so we can deal with them.

for correction,

To rectify the sin and restore the person.

for instruction in righteousness:

Our manual of Spiritual training.

That the man of God may be perfect, thoroughly furnished unto all good works.

The Bible will mature us in the faith if we choose to walk according to its statutes.

Before we leave this subject, I would recommend that you purchase a black-letter edition of the King James Bible. Many publishers place the words of Jesus in red. The words of Jesus are no more or no less important than any other portion of Scripture. The red letters give the notion that the words of Jesus hold more weight than the rest of Scripture, and this is simply not true. All Scripture is the same in authority.

Bible Study

The only way for a believer to walk in the will of God in this sin-cursed world is to know what God has to say. The Bible is God's inspired Word to us, and there is no other book on earth where the Christian can turn to find the thoughts of God. There is only one way to extract truth from the Bible, and that is to diligently study it.

Why Should I Study It?

1. So I do not sin against God—Psalm 119:9
2. So I may be equipped to do God's work—2 Timothy 3:16–17
3. So I may be rooted in sound doctrine—Ephesians 4:14
4. So I may know the truth of Christ—John 8:32
5. So I may be an approved workman—2 Timothy 2:15
6. So I may know what the will of God is for my life—Romans 12:2

Where Should I Study?

Find a quiet out-of-the-way place where the television or telephone will not bother you. You may also study while you are driving your car by listening to good quality Christian radio or you may purchase CDs of sermons and the King James Bible.

What Method should I use?

1. Topical—Anger, joy, hell, etc.
2. Book by book—To gain insight into the historical as well as the spiritual meaning.
3. Doctrinal studies—Doctrine of God, Doctrine of Christ, Doctrine of Satan, etc.
4. Word studies—Temptation, sin, will, etc.
5. Personality studies—Pick out a biblical character, like Moses, and study their life and traits. This method will show you how much like us they really were.

How Do I Approach the Bible?

1. Expectation—Expecting God to reveal truth to me.
2. Desire—Desire to know God's Word.
3. Investigative attitude—Sometimes a biblical answer may take hours or even days to find, because the truth must be pieced together.

What Bible Helps Are Available to Me?

1. Concordance—Contains all the words in the Old and New Testament along with their original language meaning. I recommend *Strong's Exhaustive Concordance*.
2. Bible Dictionary—To help understand people, places, and customs of the Bible. A good Bible dictionary helps to decipher some of the Eastern customs which seem mysterious. I recommend *Unger's Bible Dictionary*.
3. Topical Bible—Has verses listed according to topics. I recommend the *Naves Topical Bible*.
4. Bible Atlas—A Bible atlas is invaluable to Bible study because you will want to find the locations of the places named in the Bible. There are quite a number of them available.

5. Manners and Customs book—There are many things in the Scriptures which seem strange to us who live in the west. I would suggest *The New Manners and Customs of the Bible* by James Freeman.
6. Bible Almanac—A Bible Almanac will help you on many subjects such as archaeology, geography, people groups such as the Romans, languages of the Bible, Bible outlines, etc. It is a very valuable book to aid in your studies.
7. Study Bible—They contain reference verses, maps, historical knowledge, small concordances, etc. My four recommendations are in the preface.
8. Correspondence Courses—There are many colleges which offer off campus study programs for both credit and non-credit. Before you accept any courses, be sure to get a copy of their doctrinal statement. Many colleges doubt parts of the Bible.

The Golden Rule of Biblical Interpretation

The Bible is its own interpreter. This is how God meant it to be.

> Which things also we speak, not in the words which man's wisdom teacheth, but which the Holy Ghost teacheth; comparing spiritual things with spiritual. (1 Corinthians 2:13)

Do not pick up all kinds of theology books, especially prophecy books with all their fantasy, until you are sufficiently grounded in the Scriptures. Actually, when you learn the Bible by comparing Scripture with Scripture, you will want nothing to do with all these prophecy books. Everyone and their brothers are writing prophecy books today, and 99 percent of them are based on fanciful speculation.

As a young Christian, if you pick up these kind of books, you will automatically interpret the Bible according to these books instead of using the Bible to interpret them. This happened to me when I was a young Christian. These books caused me to stumble over many passages that didn't fit into the view of these books. It caused me much confusion.

When I rid myself of those books, literally, God began to clear up my biblical understanding, and difficult passages became clear. This will only happen when you let the Bible be its own interpreter. I am trying to save you the great amount of confusion which I experienced. I want to see you gain a clear understanding of Scripture as a young Christian, because when you ground yourself properly in the Scriptures, you will grow properly. One thing I can't save you from, and I don't want to, is the large amount of time you will need to study to gain a good understanding of Scripture.

If you have a computer, I highly recommend a great study tool called "Sword Searcher" which is available at https://www.swordsearcher.com/. I have been using this software for years.

Satan

The name Satan means "adversary;" in other words, he is your enemy. He cannot possess you or own you, but he will attempt to defeat you in your Christian walk. Satan cannot do anything to you unless it is allowed by God (Job 2:5–6).

The Existence of Satan

It is doubted by the world:

A. Because of all the silly cartoons which picture Satan as a two-horned, fork-tailed creature in red flannel underwear.
B. Liberal preachers have been too silent about Satan.
C. Conservative preaching has been silent about him also.
D. A quotation from the *Baptist Bulletin*, December 1971, Page 13:

> If I were the devil, the first thing I would do is deny my own existence…this disciple of doubt seems to thrive best when he is underestimated or ignored or denied… If I were the devil I would deny my existence to the world and downplay it in the local church, thus freeing me to go about my business unheeded, unhindered, and unchecked.

On April 3, 1965, a great news commentator on radio named Paul Harvey had broadcast the following message concerning Satan.

SATAN

Paul Harvey was a Christian and was on hundreds of radio stations in the majority of cities across the USA, so this message went out to millions of people.

> If I were the Devil...I mean, if I were the Prince of Darkness, I would of course, want to engulf the whole earth in darkness. I would have a third of its real estate and four-fifths of its population, but I would not be happy until I had seized the ripest apple on the tree, so I should set about however necessary to take over the United States. I would begin with a campaign of whispers. With the wisdom of a serpent, I would whisper to you as I whispered to Eve: "Do as you please." "Do as you please." To the young, I would whisper, "The Bible is a myth." I would convince them that man created God instead of the other way around. I would confide that what is bad is good, and what is good is "square." In the ears of the young marrieds, I would whisper that work is debasing, that cocktail parties are good for you. I would caution them not to be extreme in religion, in patriotism, in moral conduct. And the old, I would teach to pray. I would teach them to say after me: "Our Father, which art in Washington"
>
> If I were the devil, I'd educate authors in how to make lurid literature exciting so that anything else would appear dull and uninteresting. I'd threaten T.V. with dirtier movies and vice versa. And then, if I were the devil, I'd get organized. I'd infiltrate unions and urge more loafing and less work, because idle hands usually work for me. I'd peddle narcotics to whom I could. I'd sell alcohol to ladies and gentlemen of distinction. And I'd tranquilize the rest with pills. If I were the devil, I would encourage schools to

refine young intellects but neglect to discipline emotions…let those run wild. I would designate an atheist to front for me before the highest courts in the land and I would get preachers to say "she's right." With flattery and promises of power, I could get the courts to rule what I construe as against God and in favor of pornography, and thus, I would evict God from the courthouse, and then from the school house, and then from the houses of Congress and then, in his own churches I would substitute psychology for religion, and I would deify science because that way men would become smart enough to create super weapons but not wise enough to control them.

If I were Satan, I'd make the symbol of Easter an egg, and the symbol of Christmas, a bottle. If I were the devil, I would take from those who have and I would give to those who wanted, until I had killed the incentive of the ambitious. And then, my police state would force everybody back to work. Then, I could separate families, putting children in uniform, women in coal mines, and objectors in slave camps. In other words, if I were Satan, I'd just keep on doing what he's doing.

—Paul Harvey, *Good Day*.[2]

There are groups today who completely deny the existence of Satan because of following false teachings of others. This happens when people do not study their Scriptures and allow a central person to do all their thinking for them.

---

[2] You can hear this on YouTube at: https://www.youtube.com/watch?v=H3Az0okaHig&t=16s

The Five-Fold Sin of Satan from Isaiah 14:12–14

1. I will ascend into heaven—he wanted to rule in God's place as he desired equality with God.
2. I will exalt my throne above the stars of God—A possible reference to Satan wanting to be worshipped by the angels or the children of God.
3. I will sit upon the mount of the congregation, in the sides of the north:
   A. The mountain where God agreed to meet his people and make himself known to them. This was Sinai.
   B. Satan wanted control of the entire universe. In heathen writings, the north was the home of the ancient gods, possibly the Babylonian gods since the Book of Isaiah was written during the apostasy of the divided era of the nation of Israel.
   C. In Scripture, a mountain is a synonym for a kingdom. Satan wanted to have authority not only over his one kingdom, but also the kingdom of God. "I will lift up mine eyes unto the hills, from whence cometh my help. {2} My help cometh from the LORD, which made heaven and earth" (Psalm 121:1–2).
4. I will ascend above the heights of the clouds—he may be referring to the glory of God. (Exodus 16:10)
5. I will be like the most high—Most High is the Hebrew description of God, which means the "strongest strong one." He coveted the power of God.

Some of the Methods Satan Uses to Deceive

1. He sows tares among the wheat—Matthew 24:30—This corresponds to unbelievers existing in the local church assembly along with believers.
2. He sows false doctrine—1 Timothy 4:1–3
3. He defiles the Word of God:

A. Taking it out of context—Matthew 4:6—In this passage he quoted Psalm 91:11 but conveniently left out the part "To keep thee in all thy ways."
   B. Misinterpretation
   C. Overstressing one sided doctrine (biased interpretation)
   D. Disregards certain doctrines like the doctrine of Satan.
   E. Eisegesis—It means placing an erroneous meaning on a Scripture verse.
4. He hinders the work of God—1 Thessalonians 2:18
5. He can hinder the prayers of God's people—Daniel 10:12–13
6. He blinds people to the gospel—2 Corinthians 4:4
7. He steals the truth—Matthew 13:19
8. He is the accuser of the brethren—Revelation 12:9–10
9. He sets snares for people—2 Timothy 2:26
10. He tempts people—Matthew 4:1; Ephesians 6:11
11. He can afflict people—Job 2:7; 2 Corinthians 12:7
12. He deceives—Revelation 12:9, 20:10
13. He sabotages the home—1 Corinthians 7:5
14. He induces the sinner and saint to sin against God:
    A. David—1 Chronicles 21:1
    B. Judas—John 13:27
    C. Peter's rebuke of Jesus—Matthew 16:22–23
    D. Ananias and Sapphira—Acts 5:1–11

Satan is a defeated foe and a created being. He has no power or authority over the Christian. His power is not greater than God's power, and on the last day, he will be cast into the lake of fire along with all those who followed him and denied Christ.

The Church

The word *church* is derived from the Greek Word *kuriakos* which means "belonging to the Lord." It is found in 1 Corinthians 11:20 and Revelation 1:10.

> When ye come together therefore into one place, this is not to eat the Lord's supper. (1 Corinthians 11:20)

> I was in the Spirit on the Lord's day, and heard behind me a great voice, as of a trumpet, (Revelation 1:10)

Both uses of "Lord's" above is the word *kuriakos*. The Scottish word *Kirk* is derived from this word, and so is the English word *church*. This is why the King James translators used the word *church*, because it conveys the meaning of "belonging to the Lord." Now this means only those who are truly saved are the church and not anyone who just joins a visible assembly. One must be born again to belong to the eternal church of God.

The general Greek word behind "church, assembly, and congregation" in the New Testament is the word *ekklesia* which means a "called out assembly." The church is the living organism which Christ came to redeem and which has the mandate for sending forth the gospel. We will take a biblical look at what the church is, and you may be surprised, because differences exist between what we conceive the church to be and what the Bible says it is. The church is thought of in two different manners:

1. The Invisible Church—This constitutes all the believers which are spread throughout the world and that are not gathered into a local assembly or a single place.
2. The Visible Church—This is the local assembly which we see on Sunday morning. It is called the visible church because we can physically see the people gathered.

Symbol of the Church in the Old Testament

In Acts 7:38, while Stephen was giving his discourse about the history of Israel, he included the statement, "The church in the wilderness." Stephen was telling us that the Israelites were a called-out assembly, and this may easily be borne out by a study of Exodus. They were called out of Egypt. This represents the Christians being called out of the kingdom of Satan and placed into the kingdom of God, which is the church. Egypt, in the Bible, is a symbol of the world system. Moses was a symbol or type of Christ.

As Moses led the Israelites out of bondage, Christ leads us out of the bondage of sin and Satan. So from this, we conclude that the nation of Israel typified the church in the New Testament. The land of Canaan, which was known as the promised land, was a symbol of the kingdom of God.

Some of the Biblical Names for the Church

1. The Body of Christ—Ephesians 1:22–23
2. The Pearl of Great Price—Matthew 13:45–46
3. The Flock of God—Isaiah 40:11; 1 Peter 5:2
4. The House of God—1 Timothy 3:15
5. The Household of God—Ephesians 2:19 (family)
6. The Bride of Christ—Revelation 19:7
7. A Great Multitude—Revelation 7:9
8. Israel of God—Galatians 6:16

9. Assembly of the Saints—Psalm 89:7
10. Assembly of the Upright—Psalm 111:1
11. The Heavenly Family—Ephesians 3:15
12. God's Building; God's Husbandry—1 Corinthians 3:9
13. The Holy City—Hebrews 12:12
14. Pillar and Ground of the Truth—1 Timothy 4:15

Concerns About the Local Church

1. Not everyone who belongs to a church is saved—Matthew 13:24–30,36–40. In modern times, the church has let down its spiritual guard and allows anyone to be a member, whether they are Christians or not. Those in the church who are unsaved are represented by the tares. Those who are saved are represented by the wheat. Christ allows both to exist in the same congregation, but on the last day, as he states in vv. 30 and 39–40, he will separate them. The wheat (Christians) will go into the barn (heaven), and the tares (unbelievers) will be cast into hell.
2. Many times, Christ's goal and the church's goal are not the same. In some churches, there is a goal set just to feed the hungry and focus on social problems. This should not be the focus of the church; however, it may be part of their ministry, but it should not be the main emphasis. The sending forth of the gospel is to be the main emphasis of the church as stated in Matthew 28:19–20.
3. By joining a good Bible-believing church (there are churches who do not believe the Bible, so beware), you will be able to grow rapidly and properly in your Christian walk. So look for a good church when you begin your search. If you can find a good home Bible Study in someone's home, try to attend as this will help you in your growth. If you are unable to find a good church in your area but there are good house churches, then by all means attend. The early church met in homes. If you attend a house church, make sure you get their doctrinal statement as some have started

house churches and have turned into cults as the leaders have no spiritual discernment.
4. God designed the local church for the born-again Christian only and not for the unbeliever. They may attend but are not to have any positions of leadership. The weekly meetings are for believers to be strengthened and ministered to so they can go out into the world and fulfill the great commission.

Born Again

Now that you have become saved, you should know a little about what the biblical saying "born again" means. We hear the world use that term when someone begins a new chapter in their life, like a drug addict or drunkard who has been freed from their substance. The world states that they have been given a new lease on life or they have been born again. In 1972, John Denver released a song called "Rocky Mountain High," and in the lyrics, he sang about a man who came to the mountains, and it was like he was "born again."

As a new Christian, I want to make sure that you understand what it means to be "born again." Let me state that being born again in its truest sense is only applicable to the true Christian. No one can become born again unless God does it. The phrase may also be translated "born from above," because this is the Greek rendering assuring us that no one can become born again apart from Christ. Unless a person is born again, he or she is not a Christian.

Let us now briefly look at what the Bible has to say about this subject.

What Is Born Again?

1. Spiritual Resurrection—Ephesians 2:1

As unbelievers, we were once spiritually dead toward the things of God. We had physical life, but not spiritual life. We could not understand spiritual things. So when we were saved, our dead spirits were resurrected to life by means of the indwelling Holy Spirit (Luke 15:24; Romans 8:11; 1 Corinthians 2:14).

2. The Exchanged Life—Ezekiel 36:25–28

Now that we are living a spiritual life which is alive unto God, we will want to exchange the old habits and sins for the newness of a life that is pleasing to God. We will have the desire to be obedient to God (Ephesians 4:22–24).

Where Did It Take Place?

It took place in your soul (John 1:12–13). As you can see, you still have your existing body parts; they don't glow or change colors. You, like me, still have the same aches and pains. So it is obvious our fleshly bodies were not born again, but only our spirit was. The reason that you and I may live a Godly life is because the flesh is to obey the spirit. God gave us the Holy Spirit to indwell us and impart to us the power that is needed to overcome sinful flesh.

Why Is it Essential?

1. Man is under condemnation for sin—John 3:18,36
2. Man is helpless and cannot save himself—Ephesians 2:4–5,11–12
3. So man may properly worship God—John 4:23–24 (Lydia—Acts 16:14)
4. Man cannot inherit heaven on his own—Matthew 7:21–23; Romans 3:20; Ephesians
5. 2:8–9; Titus 3:4–5
6. To be able to accomplish true good works—Ephesians 2:10 (compare to Proverbs 21:27); true good works are only done by people after they are saved, not before.
7. To become the true children of God—Romans 8:15–16

Once I Am Saved, Can I Ever Lose My Salvation?

The answer is no, because you did nothing to earn it, so you can do nothing to lose it. Here are four reasons why you can't lose your salvation:

1. Eternal life is a gift—Romans 6:23
2. God does not recall his gifts—Romans 11:29
3. The Holy Spirit has sealed us till the day of our redemption, which is either our physical death or the return of Christ on the last day (Ephesians 4:30).
4. Eternal life begins at the moment of salvation, not our death (1 John 5:11–13). If eternal life can be lost, then it is not eternal but temporal.

There are many other reasons found in Scripture why you cannot lose your salvation, and you will come across them as you read and study your Bible. There are many who teach that you can lose your salvation, and this is because they do not understand God's salvation plan. The loss of salvation is contrary to the Bible and should not be heeded. Those who teach it are living in a "work for salvation" gospel, and if they are, then it is obvious they are unsaved also. Grace and grace alone!

Angels

The word *angel* is translated from the Greek word *aggelos* (pronounced "angelos") which means "messenger." It is used in this form in the entire New Testament except for Luke 20:36 in the phrase "equal unto the angels," where the word *isaggelos* is used, which means "like an angel, angelic." They are also referred to in Scripture as "The Host." Remember one of God's names is "Lord of Hosts."

There are some people and groups who completely deny the existence of angels, simply because they do not understand that angels are a mysterious group of spirit beings whom God uses in different ways and situations. The bottom line is that angels are real, and those who deny their existence are literally calling God a liar because of the many Scriptures which speak of angels. By denying parts of the Bible, they are showing their salvation status, and that is they are unsaved.

Biblical Facts About the Angels

1. Hebrews 1:14—Angels are spirits that minister to Christ (Psalm 68:17; Matthew 4:11).
2. Nehemiah 9:6—They were created by God and Christ.
3. Hebrews 1:6—The angels worship Christ.
4. Luke 1:19—They deliver communication from God.
5. Psalm 103:20—They obey the commandments of God and are mighty in strength.
6. Genesis 19:13—They execute the judgment of God.

7. Matthew 16:27—They will accompany Christ at his second coming.
8. Luke 15:10—They rejoice when a person becomes saved.
9. Psalm 91:11—They protect the Christian.
10. Colossians 2:18—They are not to be worshipped; this is forbidden (Deuteronomy 17:2–3; Jeremiah 8:1–3)
11. 2 Samuel 14:20—They have wisdom.
12. 2 Peter 2:11—They are meek.
13. Matthew 25:31—They are holy.
14. 1 Timothy 5:21—They are elect.
15. Hebrew 12:22—There are countless numbers of them.
16. Matthew 24:31—They will gather all the elect unto Christ on the last day.

God's Requirements for Christians

1. Read and Study your Bible—Psalm 119:11,105
2. Have a daily prayer life—1 Thessalonians 5:17
3. Attend a good Bible-believing church—Hebrews 10:24–25
4. Give money to the Lord's work—2 Corinthians 8:11–12; Deuteronomy 16:17
5. Give yourself to some phase of the Lord's work—Romans 12:1
6. Refuse to partake in the old sins which God has delivered you from—Romans 12:2
7. Get to know Christ, because too many Christians know about him, but they do not know him intimately—Matthew 11:28–30
8. Be a witness to the gospel and personally spread the gospel to friends, family, and even those you do not know personally—Matthew 24:14; Mark 16:15

Some Realities of the Christian Life We Must Face:

1. We will be rejected by some people—Matthew 12:14
2. Not every Christian will be in agreement with other Christians—Acts 15:36–41
3. Satan will tempt us, but God will give us a way of escape—1 Corinthians 10:13
4. We will be misunderstood—John 3:3–7
5. All your problems will not go away, but sometimes they intensify—Philippians 2:7

6. Sometimes we will sin against God because we still have bodies which lust after sin—2 Samuel 12:13

Don't get scared, because it is a wonderful life; but too many portray it as one big "high" when it isn't. This is why when tough times come, these people are the first to fail, because they are unprepared. As you begin your walk with God, you will see that the problems which once seemed paramount will look like a molehill in comparison to the majesty of God.

Giving with Wisdom

Every man according as he purposeth in his heart,
so let him give; not grudgingly, or of necessity:
for God loveth a cheerful giver.
—2 Corinthians 9:7

One of the dynamics of the Christian life which I learned as a young Christian was the giving of finances to ministries and missions which were sending forth the Gospel. Of course, we are commanded to go into all the world and preach the Gospel.

> And he said unto them, "Go ye into all the world, and preach the gospel to every creature." (Mark 16:15)

Let us be realistic—not every Christian will go to a different country and be a missionary. God has saved millions of Christians and kept them right where they were saved.

> And when he was come into the ship, he that had been possessed with the devil prayed him that he might be with him. {19} Howbeit Jesus suffered him not, but saith unto him, "Go home to thy friends, and tell them how great things the Lord hath done for thee, and hath had compassion on thee." (Mark 5:18–19)

GIVING WITH WISDOM

The Gadarene Demoniac was such a person. Once Jesus had freed him from all those devils which possessed him, he felt so much love for Jesus that he desired to follow him in ministry. Instead, we read in the above verses that Jesus did not allow him to come with them but sent him home to his family and friends to be a witness to them.

This is what happens to the majority of Christians when they become newly saved. God returns them to their homes, and they become a witness right where they are. There is another reason why God allows that: because many Christians work, and when a person works, they can finance ministries to send forth the Gospel. That Christian now has the opportunity to be a witness for Jesus right where they work and live.

> But Jesus said unto them, "A prophet is not without honour, but in his own country, and among his own kin, and in his own house." (Mark 6:4)

Witnessing to people who knew you and the things you did before salvation is one of the toughest ministries a Christian can have, but if they continue properly in the Christian life, people will eventually have to acknowledge there is definitely a change.

This chapter is about using wisdom in giving money to ministries. God has allowed some Christians to gain great wealth in this world. Some names that come to mind are R. G. Letourneau, Colgate, Welch's Grape Juice, and there are no doubt others.

However, the normal pattern is that most Christians who God saves are workers who work for someone else and draw a paycheck. So this Christian wants to make sure that what they are giving is actually being used to further the kingdom of God on earth. This is where it is absolutely necessary to use wisdom when giving, because with limited funds, you want to make sure that your gift has maximum impact for the Gospel.

There are many false preachers out there, and it seems the majority of them are on TV. One of them has a net worth of about $20 million and brags that he has three Corvettes. That is not where you want your hard-earned money winding up. We are responsible before the Lord to be wise stewards of the money he has entrusted to us.

> Moreover it is required in stewards, that a man be found faithful. (1 Corinthians 4:2)

Notice that the verse says it is "required" that a steward be found faithful; it does not say it is an option. I would like to share with you some principles of wise giving which I have learned over the last thirty-nine years of being saved.

When desiring to give, it is always a good practice to investigate the mission or ministry to make sure your donation is not falling into a black hole. With the advent of the Internet, this is possible. When seeking to support a certain ministry, there should be some basic questions which you must ask. Keep in mind that the Bible teaches that we are to be wise stewards of the Lord's money. You may have a desire to give to a ministry which does general evangelism through teaching or preaching, or maybe a literature ministry or a shortwave radio ministry or even an Internet ministry, and that is why you need to be an informed giver.

What is the Focus of the Ministry?

A focus is "A central point; point of concentration" according to the 1828 Webster Dictionary. This is where you match up your desire with their ministry. You may have a desire to reach a certain area of the world by shortwave, so you would check out some shortwave ministries to see where they broadcast to. Say you would like to reach South America, then you might want to support (Reach Beyond) HCJB which is headquartered in Quito, Ecuador. They had their start in 1931, which tells you that this ministry has been sending forth the Gospel for eighty-eight years as of 2019.

Now you will want to know what the focus of their ministry is, such as, is it evangelism, teaching, discipleship, Bible translation, literacy (teaching people how to read), or other ministries? Let us say the focus of their ministry is evangelism; so with that being the focus, then you would be investing the Lord's money wisely in that ministry. You would be partnering (and that is what it is) with a ministry sending forth the Gospel for twenty-four hours per day, seven days per week.

What Is Their Method of Ministry?

You may be a writer or even an avid reader of books and would like to invest in a literature ministry. You could look at World Missionary Press who publishes Bible booklets in more than 345 languages. Now you may not be concerned about reaching a specific people group, but you have a heart's desire to reach many. So you could invest with them on a monthly basis and just check the box "Where Needed Most" and let the Lord direct them where to use the funds. One month, you might be helping to send booklets to India, and another month to Cuba.

> Cast thy bread upon the waters: for thou shalt
> find it after many days. (Ecclesiastes 11:1)

This is truly a fulfillment of the meaning of Ecclesiastes 11:1. You might be an airplane pilot and want to support an aviation ministry, so you might want to check out JAARS which flies missionaries and ministry materials around in a fleet of small planes. You may also want to partner with a missions ministry which still sends missionaries to different parts of the world. You may like the idea of presenting the Gospel in a dramatic way, so you might want to support Unshackled from Pacific Garden Mission or Lamplighter Theater. So it is always good to find out what method the ministry uses to send forth the Gospel, because that would be a main emphasis and expense of the ministry.

There are some ministries out there which send Bibles free of charge to people as the money comes in. One such ministry is Bible for Today which sends Bibles to prisoners on request, and people can donate to that fund and partner in this ministry. Another such ministry is Bearing Precious Seed that publishes quality King James Bibles, and many are sent overseas. So you can support ministries which produce Bibles. There is a Bible shortage in the world, and this would be another great ministry to support because it fills in the needs for so many indigenous preachers in other countries. Many times, there may be only one Bible for an entire village.

Where Do They Minister?

There are going to be many missionary organizations which have a single focus on one area of the world. Sometimes they will focus only on one country or a region, such as Gospel for Asia. One such single-focus ministry is China Inland Mission which was started in 1865 and is now called OMF International and has a focus on East Asia. There are missionary organizations which focus on Africa, the Middle East, Europe, and individual countries. You may have a burden for a certain country and want to support ministry in that country. It is always important to know where a specific ministry ministers so you will be well-informed as to where your donation will be ministering.

How Long Have They Been in Ministry?

We have to be very careful here, because with the advent of the Internet, there are people who set up ministries and throw "donate buttons" on the site and never plan to use any of the donated money for ministry. My website has been online for over twenty-one years, and I will not place a donate button on my site. If someone wants to donate, they can contact me, and I will give them the particulars.

There are some ministries which have been operating continually for many years, and it is very safe to support them. We mentioned China Inland Mission which was started in 1865, then there is the Salvation Army which began in 1865, the Pacific Garden Mission which started in 1877, Africa Inland Mission which began in 1895, and Every Home for Christ started in 1946. A ministry that has been around for a long time is normally a good investment of funds but with longevity in ministry can come creeping liberalism which can water down the truth of the Gospel. If you choose to support a ministry which has been around a long time, then investigate if they are still proclaiming the true Gospel in all its strength. Read their materials or listen to their programs to check them out.

How Much Salary Do the Leaders Draw?

This is important, because in many false ministries, the leaders draw salaries of hundreds of thousands to millions of dollars. This is not only a problem in the charismatic movement, but also in other ministries and some churches. You can check what some ministries are paying their leaders by going to the following site: https://www.charitynavigator.org.

High salaries taken out of donations means for these ministries a good portion of donations go to high salaries. Now, there is nothing wrong about paying decent salaries in a ministry, because people have to live and pay bills, but when they get into six figures, that is just wrong. Then these same ministries cry the blues that they need money for every pet project and yet will not reduce the high salaries of the CEO. This is why when you are seeking out a ministry to support, it is important to know their salary philosophy, because if they are in it for salaries, then the ministry needs will suffer, and when donations come in, it will be directed into the salary needs.

There is one thing I like about the salary philosophy of World Missionary Press and that is all employees make the same pay from the president to the pressman. That is how ministry should be done and is a great example of wise stewardship.

What Partnerships Have They Formed?

A real good partnership is World Missionary Press partnering with Every Home for Christ to evangelize as many places as possible using WMP materials. This is very important, because the wrong partnership can affect the quality of the ministry and the very message itself. Some ministries may partner with environmental groups or even the Roman Catholic Church, which is not a Christian church and does not teach the truth. It is good to know what organizations or people your target ministry is involved with, because you may be helping a false religion.

This is why you must be informed as to what you are giving to. Let me give you a personal example. When I was a new Christian, I was giving $10 a month to Salesian Missions. I did not find out until a few months later that they were Roman Catholic, and as soon as I found out, they did not get one penny from me again.

What About Smaller Ministries?

So far, I have only mentioned larger ministries, but there are also smaller ministries out there which are doing a great job in evangelizing. There is a woman named Debbie Carver here in New Jersey who operates a small ministry called Our Father's Persistent Love Ministries, which is a ministry to prisoners. Her ministry has had great effect upon many prisoners. A small ministry with a focus like that is well-worth supporting.

There are many small ministries on the Internet which need to be approached with caution, because many have started them just to raise money for personal use. Just because a ministry only has one or two people in it does not mean it is not playing an important role in the lives of those it comes in contact with. Technology has made it easy to do ministry and has cut down the need for much office space or personnel. One or two people today can handle what five or six did twenty years ago. Smaller ministries should never be overlooked, because their outreach is just as important as those of the larger ministries. For example, my own personal website is viewed in over 150 countries every month. That is a tremendous outreach for only one person.

Beware of the Hook

You will hear from some ministries, especially the charismatic ministries on TV, that if you send them $1,000, then God will bless you with health and wealth. Do not fall for this satanic scheme! Many of them interview people in the audience and tell of how God has blessed them because they made a $1,000 faith pledge to their ministry. These are shills! A shill is one who acts as a decoy being in league with the ministry or minister they are promoting. The money that goes to these types of ministries normally goes into buying mansions or personal jets for the preacher.

Beware when you hear these false preachers talk about "seed money." There is no such thing as seed money in the Bible. I wish to name some false teachers who are only in it for the money and, therefore, you should steer clear of them: Ken Copeland, T. D. Jakes, Joseph Prince, Joyce Meyer, Joel Osteen, Jesse Duplantis, Creflo Dollar, Paula White, Rod Parsley, Andrew Wommack, Marilyn Hickey, Bill Winston, John Hagee, Peter Popoff, Kenneth Hagin, Sid Roth, etc.

There is nothing wrong making a faith pledge because of your desire to send forth the Gospel. If you do, pick a reputable ministry like World Missionary Press or JAARS and send them a gift every month toward your faith pledge.

> But this I say, he which soweth sparingly shall reap also sparingly; and he which soweth bountifully shall reap also bountifully. {7} Every man according as he purposeth in his heart, so let him give; not grudgingly, or of necessity: for God loveth a cheerful giver. {8} And God is able to make all grace abound toward you; that ye, always having all sufficiency in all things, may abound to every good work: (2 Corinthians 9:6–8)

Now, it is true that God does bless in response to a person's giving and their attitude toward the giving, but he does so in different ways and not necessarily health and wealth. He may increase your finances as you go along or he may not. Instead, he might keep you from an accident or a sickness which could cause you to lose pay. However he does it, he does promise that he will bless the giver.

Summary

Giving is a great dynamic of the Christian Faith. Our money can get the word of God into places that we cannot go. As with anything in life, we must be very discerning as to where we send the money which we earn by the sweat of our brow. We want it to advance the Christian faith and not go into someone's pocket. We are to make an impact in this world with the Gospel, and evangelism is one way of invading Satan's territory. The more people hear the true Gospel, the more will respond.

Once the last one becomes saved, which God has named, then the end shall come. If the money we send is sequestered in someone's bank account, then that money is dead for the spread of the Gospel. Let me once again reference World Missionary Press. They can manufacture twenty-five Gospel booklets for every dollar received. If you are able to just send $10 a month, that means you would be able to reach 250 people a month that you would otherwise be unable to reach. Multiply that by twelve months, and you will have reached 3,000 people plus in different countries. The people who receive the booklets will share with others, thus multiplying your gift further. So when you give unto the Lord, he will not only bless you but will multiply the outreach of the materials you fund. It is a great partnership, and that is why it is important to do your homework and investigate the ministry or mission you desire to support.

Ministries Mentioned in This Chapter in a Positive Light:

Africa Inland Mission—https://aimint.org/
Bearing Precious Seed—http://www.bpsmilford.org/
Bible for Today—http://www.biblefortoday.org/
Every Home for Christ—http://www.ehc.org/
JAARS—https://jaars.org/
Lamplighter Theater—https://www.lamplightertheatre.com/
OMF International—https://omf.org/
Our Father's Persistent Love Ministries—http://ofpl.org/

Pacific Garden Mission—https://www.pgm.org/
Reach Beyond (Formerly HCJB)—https://reachbeyond.org/
Salvation Army—http://www.salvationarmy.org/
World Missionary Press—http://www.wmpress.org/

Giving: A Dynamic of the Christian Life

How Shall We Give?

> I am the LORD thy God, which brought thee out of the
> land of Egypt: open thy mouth wide, and I will fill it.
> —Psalm 81:10

Now that you have read about how to give with wisdom, in this chapter, I want to give you the dynamics of giving finances to ministry and what a powerful ministry it really is. The Christian dynamic of giving has been so muddied by the church that instead of it being a part of worship as it should be, it becomes a "calculating event." You will hear the following questions in reference to giving:

- Do I give 10 percent?
- Do I tithe on the gross?
- Do I tithe on the net?
- Is tithing a New Testament principle?
- Is tithing demanded by God?
- If we are under grace, why do we have to tithe?

Depending on the church you attend, you will continue to hear these debates about giving. Giving is a great part of the Great Commission. It funds the going forth of world missions. However, keep in mind that if God is calling you to the mission field, then giving money to missions in lieu of going yourself is unacceptable, and you will not get away with it (Read Jonah chapter 1).

When I first became a Christian in 1980, the man who discipled me put into my heart a love for missions. Since I have two bad knees, I was unable to go to a mission field. I supported missions and still do. I have a heart for missionaries, because the ones that I have come in contact with have given their entire lives to sending forth the gospel.

There is one thing I want to bring up at this point. When you find a mission agency to support and you receive an envelope with a short form to fill out, asking what you want to donate to, and you are not sure, then do not be afraid to check the box "Where Needed Most" or "General Expenses." Many do not give unless it goes to some mission deep in the jungles of Irian Jaya or some other exotic place. God will take the money you donate, and it will be used in the right place, so don't fear that you are displeasing God if you check "Where Needed most."

World Missionary Press in Indiana does this. They list several projects, plus the "Where Needed Most" option. I always check that one, because they know better where the money is needed most.

That was an aside, yet it is a very important subject concerning giving to missions. That is what this chapter is all about. I hope to clear up some confusion about giving, because I see it is a great dynamic of the Christian walk. Let me share a personal incident with you which happened because of God's faithfulness to his word when we give.

Back in the 1980s, I received a letter from one of my favorite ministries which was $30,000 behind in bills. I remember I had $2,000 in a savings account. The Lord had laid upon my heart to give $1,000 to this ministry. So I did it, and shortly thereafter, a relative of mine gave me about $2,500 in Savings Bonds in face value she was saving for me since 1954. I took them to the bank and cashed them in. The total came out to about $5,500. God had graciously and faithfully kept his Word concerning the promises of giving. I have another personal giving incident which I will share later in the study.

Remember the verse which I started this study with? Psalm 81:10. I first heard this principle enunciated by Dr. Charles Stanley back in the early '80s when I was a young Christian. The question is, how wide are you willing to open your mouth so the Lord can fill it? This simply means, are you willing to take God at his Word and trust him by giving generously (open wide)? Or to be stingy and give little (open slightly)?

It was John Wesley who said:

- Make all you can!
- Save all you can!
- Give all you can!

Basically, what Wesley was saying is there must be balance in the Christian financial walk. God does not expect you to place your whole pay in the collection plate, because he knows there are legitimate living expenses and emergencies which arise. Please keep this principle in mind: God will never use your money as an instrument to entrap you, but he will use it to test your faithfulness to him.

Let us now attend to the words of Scripture which God gives that deal with the subject of giving. We will look at 2 Corinthians 9:6–15 as our starting point, and then we will expand the study to many different verses which detail the dynamic of giving:

> {6} But this I say, he which soweth sparingly shall reap also sparingly; and he which soweth bountifully shall reap also bountifully. {7} Every man according as he purposeth in his heart, so let him give; not grudgingly, or of necessity: for God loveth a cheerful giver. {8} And God is able to make all grace abound toward you; that ye, always having all sufficiency in all things, may abound to every good work: {9} (As it is written, he hath dispersed abroad; he hath given to the poor: his righteousness remaineth forever. {10} Now he that ministereth seed to the sower both minister bread for your food, and multiply your seed sown, and increase the fruits of your righteousness;) {11} Being enriched in every thing to all bountifulness, which causeth through us

thanksgiving to God. {12} For the administration of this service not only supplieth the want of the saints, but is abundant also by many thanksgivings unto God; {13} Whiles by the experiment of this ministration they glorify God for your professed subjection unto the gospel of Christ, and for your liberal distribution unto them, and unto all men; {14} And by their prayer for you, which long after you for the exceeding grace of God in you. {15} Thanks be unto God for his unspeakable gift. (2 Corinthians 9:6–15)

We are going to primarily focus on verses 6–8, but I wanted to include the entire context.

Verses 6–8 contain three principles of Godly giving:

Vs. 6—Principle of Sowing
Vs. 7—Principle of Attitude
Vs. 8—Principle of Return

Vs. 6—Principle of Sowing

Not Health, Wealth, Name It, and Claim It

One of the key principles of giving is to realize that it is not health, wealth, name it, and claim it. We do not give God $10 and then hold out our hands and expect to get $100. A blessing for giving may not come for years or it may come immediately. We give because we love God and want to send forth the gospel, not to further our own interests. Our responsibility is to be faithful in giving and leave the blessings to God.

Bountiful Giving

Another key principle of giving is bountiful giving. If we are to reap bountifully, then we are to sow bountifully. The Greek word in verse 6 for bountiful is *eulogias* which means "blessings." Literally, it states if you sow blessings, you will reap blessings. There are hardly any blessings in being cheap. How many blessings do you gather from cheap people?

According to What One Has

"Every man shall give as he is able, according to the blessing of the LORD thy God which he hath given thee" (Deuteronomy 16:17).

God has set different economic standards for each Christian. One Christian may make one deal and make millions while another one may never make more than $200 per week for their entire life. Why this seeming great imbalance? All I know is that God sets the economic pattern for each Christian with perfect knowledge. The Bible tells us that each Christian is to give according to what God has supplied in their life. God does not expect you to give as much as a millionaire can give.

In other words, if you don't have it to give, God is not forcing you to use your credit card to make a donation. Sometimes the person who has the lesser amount of money gives more. How? A cheap millionaire earns one million dollars per year and gives $10,000 to his church, which equals 1 percent. The person making $10,000 per year gives $1,000, which equals 10 percent. So who gave the most? In the eyes of the world, the millionaire, but in the eyes of God and in simple mathematics, the person who gave the $1,000. Why? Because 10 percent is a bigger portion than 1 percent.

So who sowed the blessings? Let me encourage you who read this. I have several millionaires in my extended family, and they don't even want to know my name. They have done nothing to help me send forth the gospel. It was the poor people who helped when needed. Millionaires give to organizations where they can gain control and gain monetary advantage. I have yet to meet one who gives in secret.

Scattering

"There is that scattereth, and yet increaseth; and there is that withholdeth more than is meet, but it tendeth to poverty" (Proverbs 11:24).

Scattering is another principle of giving. Many pastors teach that you need to bring your entire giving or just your tithe into the storehouse which they teach is the local church (I will address this later). A better principle of giving is to scatter your giving.

The word *scattereth* in our verse simply means to "disperse abroad." Basically, this verse is telling us that centralized giving is not the only way to give. God tells us to scatter or divide our giving when there is need in different areas. Remember when I said about the "Where Needed Most" box on the reply form? Well, here is where it can apply. Giving in different areas is as biblical as putting the entire amount in the collection plate, which is not wrong, provided your church is dispersing it properly.

You may have $50 to give each week, so instead of giving it to one place, you may send $20 to missions, $15 to radio ministry, and $15 for your church. You are being biblical, because you are dispersing the money for the kingdom. The second part of this verse tells of a person who refuses to give and will end up in poverty. A person who is cheap with the Lord's money is also revealing spiritual poverty. If a person refuses to give to the Lord's work, then they are exuding a certain uselessness in other areas too.

Cast Upon the Water

"Cast thy bread upon the waters: for thou shalt find it after many days" (Ecclesiastes 11:1).

This verse carries the same principle as Proverbs 11:24, but I do not want to focus on that. I want to focus on the verb *Cast* which is a Piel verb in the Hebrew which shows an intense or intentional action. Giving should be an intentional and intense action on the part of a Christian. One need not have the gift of giving to send forth the gospel. Giving to God's work should be a budgeted item akin to savings. We should not have the attitude of "Oh, here comes the plate, let me give $5." If that is all you can afford, then give it, but if you can afford more, then intentionally budget it to give. When I was out in industry, giving was part of my budget. I learned early in my Christian walk about the benefits of giving.

Let me give you another praise example of how God faithfully keeps his word. Keep in mind the following verse as I tell you this story.

> "For my thoughts are not your thoughts, neither are your ways my ways," saith the LORD. (Isaiah 55:8)

In February of 1998, I was laid off from a $30,000 per year job. My unemployment ran out at the end of August. I obtained a temporary full-time job shuttling cars for Avis. My average take-home pay was about $180. My car needed about $2,000 worth of repairs on it which included a new engine. Keep in mind I have to live on that small amount, so saving any substantial amount was out of the question at that time. I was with another driver at our Cranford, New Jersey station and spotted a car which was being sold for $1,200. The body was in excellent shape, and the engine ran well. It had 81,000 miles on it (my old car had 156,500). I told the fellow at the station that if the owner would take $1,000 for it, I would buy it. She took the $1,000, and I had a car in decent shape.

God allowed me to lose a good paying job, plus I was now two months past my last unemployment check, now with a job paying about 60 percent of what I was getting on unemployment, and it was at that time that God got me that car. I was able to afford the $1,000 with no problem. Oh, the car was fully loaded!

Here is the principle I want to bring forth. If you are faithful in giving, then God is faithful in giving! Learn this well—*you cannot out give the Lord!*

Secret Giving

"But when thou doest alms, let not thy left hand know what thy right hand doeth" (Matthew 6:3).

Giving just to get a tax deductible receipt is not giving. Giving, no matter how secret, is giving. God sees openly every time you give in secret. There may be people in your own church who need help. They are a mission field too. Some people adopt the idea that if their money is not going to the mission field, then it is not giving. Let me give you a principle to live by. A Christian in your congregation who has financial needs should be just as much a recipient of funds as a missionary organization or church.

I believe God allows certain Christians in a local congregation to have financial needs so it can be a testing ground for others in the congregation to see how they will respond to their needs.

> But whoso hath this world's good, and seeth his brother have need, and shutteth up his bowels of compassion from him, how dwelleth the love of God in him? {18} My little children, let us not love in word, neither in tongue; but in deed and in truth. (1 John 3:17–18)

If you have someone in your congregation that has need, and you know about it and have the finances to bring some relief, then do it. You will be blessed by the Lord, because the parameters of giving are not rigorously defined in Scripture. In other words, meet legitimate needs when you can, but don't advertise it. The desire to advertise your good deed may be a testing ground for you. Pass or fail?

Regular Giving

"Upon the first day of the week let every one of you lay by him in store, as God hath prospered him, that there be no gatherings when I come" (1 Corinthians 16:2).

Here, God tells us that not only should our giving be in secret or intentional, but it needs to be a systematic giving. Do not wait till you get some set amount saved to give. You should give on a weekly, monthly, or some methodical fashion. Sometimes if we save to give a large amount, if a bill arises, guess which part of the budget will get tapped for it? You guessed it, money slated for sending forth of the gospel.

Vs. 7—Principle of Attitude

> Every man according as he purposeth in his heart, so let him give; not grudgingly, or of necessity: for God loveth a cheerful giver. (2 Corinthians 9:7)

Not Grudgingly

This word literally means "sorrow, sadness, pain of mind or body." If someone has to grudgingly put $10 in the plate, then don't do it. God can make the $5 of the willing giver go farther than the $10 of the grudging giver. If you hate to part with your money, then don't fake altruism in church, just to show someone you give. God reads the heart, and if giving causes you sorrow, then keep it. Did you ever hear of car problems, house problems, medical problems, dental problems, bank failures, stock market crashes, or corrections? God can protect the finances of a willing giver, but the grudging giver is on his own.

How much do I trust God? Am I willing to commit my funds to his work and his keeping? Or do I think I can do a better job? Ask yourself the question, if I cannot trust God with money, then how can I trust him for eternal salvation? One of the great dynamics of the Christian faith is the willingness to trust God with all my possessions.

Purposeth

The word *purposeth* is a middle-voice verb which means "decide." A person who decides can go either way. God expects each

Christian to decide in his or her heart to do the right thing. If you purpose to give, then you will give with joy; but if you purpose not to give, then just to join the crowd, you will give with a grudging or with an unholy spirit toward giving. The decision for giving should have been made way before Sunday rolled around. If you wait till Sunday to see how much you have left over to give, then you are a grudging giver, which is an ungodly attitude.

A Willing Mind

"For if there be first a willing mind, it is accepted according to that a man hath, and not according to that he hath not" (2 Corinthians 8:12).

The words "willing mind" may also be translated "readiness." We should always have a ready mind when it comes to giving. We need to be ready to respond to those persons or ministries that have need. Notice in this verse, God carries a principle from Deuteronomy 16:17. God does not place any unreachable burden on any Christian. He simply expects us to give according to what he has supplied to a person.

Let me just reiterate what I said previously: God does not expect us to give on credit or way above what we can afford. If God has you earning a certain amount, then do not give above what you can "joyously" afford or else it may become grudge-giving. If all you can afford to give is $5, then give it and do not be ashamed. God can do much with a small offering when given in the right spirit.

Keep in mind what the Lord did with the loaves and fishes (Matthew 14:16–21). He took a minimal offering and turned it into a massive distribution. He will do this with any small offering. Does $1 sound like a small offering? Sure it does. Let us mention World Missionary Press in Indiana again. They can print twenty-five Bible tracts for that amount. Now give $5 to WMP, and you have 125 tracts. Now give $10 to MP, and you have 250 tracts. Two hundred and fifty tracts sometimes may be enough to evangelize an entire small village in another country. Still think $10 a month is an ineffective amount to give? Don't let Satan deceive you into thinking that way.

Stewardship Requirement

"Let a man so account of us, as of the ministers of Christ, and stewards of the mysteries of God. {2} Moreover it is required in stewards, that a man be found faithful" (1 Corinthians 4:1–2).

One thing we Christians must keep in mind is that we are stewards and not owners. If we owned everything we had, then how come we cannot take it with us? Everything we have has been given to us by God and is on loan. This is why I cannot figure out why some Christians are cheap with the Lord's money. They act like it is theirs. As a steward, we must keep in mind that we are not owners; we act on behalf of the owner of the goods. If God gives wealth to a Christian, it is not so they can buy a big house with a pool and two Cadillacs. They have it so they can dispense it as there is need.

The problem is that many clergy and church leaders bow the knee to wealthy Christians, not realizing that if they are hoarding it or are cheap with it, they are in rebellion to God. Rebellion to God is not always visible sin, like drinking highballs or six-packs of beer; it is also being tightfisted with God's money. Let's make a social comparison to illustrate this principle.

Can you picture a slave in Roman times taking his master's money and building a big house with two gold chariots in the driveway for himself, and when the master needed to distribute some money, the slave refusing to do it? Have you ever heard of the chopping block? That slave would be executed in a minute as a rebellious slave. As Christians, we must never think in that same rebellious manner concerning the money God has entrusted to us.

Gift of Giving

"Or he that exhorteth, on exhortation: he that giveth, let him do it with simplicity; he that ruleth, with diligence; he that showeth mercy, with cheerfulness" (Romans 12:8).

The person with the gift of giving lives to give. If a person gives a regular tithe or offering, this does not mean a person has the gift of giving. The one who has the gift of giving seeks opportunities to give. They look for ways to support the Gospel. They will even help out brethren who are in dire financial circumstances.

Usually, those with the gift of giving have the ability to make a good income so they can continue to give. These people also encourage others to put their money in forwarding the Gospel. These people are not stingy with God's money since they have been empowered, through their spiritual gift, to give with joy. The word *simplicity* carries with it the meaning of "generosity and purity." In other words, there is pure motive in giving.

Faithful in Least

"And I say unto you, 'Make to yourselves friends of the mammon of unrighteousness; that, when ye fail, they may receive you into everlasting habitations. {10} he that is faithful in that which is least is faithful also in much: and he that is unjust in the least is unjust also in much. {11} If therefore ye have not been faithful in the unrighteous mammon, who will commit to your trust the true riches'" (Luke 16:9–11)?

Here God makes a simple comparison. If you are too stingy to give money to God's work, then how can God trust you with the words of eternal life? In other words, you will be unfaithful in the ministry. Giving money is the easiest thing to do, yet it is the hardest thing for most Christians to do. If we are too cheap to give to God's work, then how can we expect him to place us in the ministry?

Have you ever had a test like the following which I have faced many times? Years ago, I had gone into gas stations with my employer's vehicles and filled them up and had requested a receipt. Some attendants had made them out for more than I paid. I could have turned them in to my employer, and he would have never known the difference. That is the principle—unfaithful in little, you will be unfaithful in much. Faithful in little, you will be faithful in much. Do you have young children? Have you taught them to put even a nickel in the plate or maybe only two cents? The amount does not matter, but they would be in training to be faithful in little so they can be faithful in much later on.

Vs. 8—Principle of Return

> And God is able to make all grace abound toward you; that ye, always having all sufficiency in all things, may abound to every good work. (2 Corinthians 9:8)

One thing we can count on is the faithfulness of God in all areas of life and not just finances. There is a principle of return associated with giving. I must tell you that the return may not come when you expect it; rather, it may come when you need it or unexpectedly. The following verses will help us look at the principle of return for faithful giving.

How Wide Will We Open?

"I am the LORD thy God, which brought thee out of the land of Egypt: open thy mouth wide, and I will fill it. {11} But my people would not hearken to my voice; and Israel would none of me" (Psalm 81:10–11).

Remember our opening verse. God will bless according to how much we trust him with the finances he has entrusted to us. I am not speaking of "name it and claim it;" rather, I am speaking of pure giving motives. If God sees little faith in the area of finances (closed mouth), there will be little blessing. If God sees big faith in the area of finances (wide-open mouth), then there will be an abundant blessing.

I believe God blesses us according to our attitude of the gift and not toward the amount given. Man looks on the outward, but God looks on the inward (1 Samuel 16:7).

Generous Soul Blessed

"The liberal soul shall be made fat: and he that watereth shall be watered also himself. {26} he that withholdeth corn, the people shall curse him: but blessing shall be upon the head of him that selleth it" (Proverbs 11:25–26).

The word *liberal* carries with it the meaning of "bless." Basically, the Bible is saying that the soul that blesses others will be made fat. "Fat" means to be satisfied or anointed. Here is a great principle that when one is faithful in giving or blessing others, they shall be satisfied.

> The meek shall eat and be satisfied: they shall praise the LORD that seek him: your heart shall live forever. (Psalm 22:26)

> They shall not be ashamed in the evil time: and in the days of famine they shall be satisfied. (Psalm 37:19)

> My soul shall be satisfied as with marrow and fatness; and my mouth shall praise thee with joyful lips: (Psalm 63:5)

As we jump back to our verse, Proverbs 11:26, notice God says that those who withhold will be cursed. Have you met any cheap Christians yet if you are in a church? How well are they loved for their cheapness? There are only two kinds of people who like cheap people:

A. Another cheap person.
B. Relatives who are in the cheap person's will.

Will Be Repaid

"He that hath pity upon the poor lendeth unto the LORD; and that which he hath given will he pay him again" (Proverbs 19:17).

Here is another principle of giving. When we give to the poor, let us define who the poor are. The poor are those who are unsaved. When we send forth the gospel, we are reaching those who are spiritually poor, and if they are God's elect and become saved, then they are rich. God is saying that when we give to his work, we are lending unto the Lord, and we will receive blessing at some time in the future.

Let me also add that helping those who are poor in material goods of this world is not an unbiblical act unless it begins to siphon off the money intended to send forth the gospel. We are not commanded to feed the poor with physical food, but we are to remain sensitive to the needs of people. We are commanded to feed the poor with spiritual food. The Great Commission is intended to further the gospel, but if a meal comes with it, that's okay too.

Blessings

"He that hath a bountiful eye shall be blessed; for he giveth of his bread to the poor" (Proverbs 22:9).

The word *bountiful* carries with it the meaning of "cheerful, good, or goodly." The person which makes their goods and money available for the Lord's work shall be blessed. Notice the word *shall* be blessed. There is no getting around it; those who give will be a blessed people.

Treated Generously

"But the liberal deviseth liberal things; and by liberal things shall he stand" (Isaiah 32:8).

The word *liberal* here means "generous" and carries with it the meaning that those who are generous with the Lord's money will be treated generously.

The Size of the Windows Are Proportionate

"Bring ye all the tithes into the storehouse, that there may be meat in mine house, and prove me now herewith, saith the LORD of hosts, if I will not open you the windows of heaven, and pour you out a blessing, that there shall not be room enough to receive it" (Malachi 3:10).

This verse is the most famous verse in the Bible concerning tithing. I think it is preached by every preacher in a stewardship message. There is much meat in this verse, and I think it behooves us to investigate it.

A. Tithes

Many preachers stress tithing as a mandatory part of the believer's life. I do not believe this, but they are on the right track as the tithe is a great level to begin planned giving. Before the Sinai law was given, there was tithing by two great patriarchs:

Jacob

"And this stone, which I have set for a pillar, shall be God's house: and of all that thou shalt give me I will surely give the tenth unto thee" (Gen. 28:22).

Abraham

"To whom also Abraham gave a tenth part of all; first being by interpretation King of righteousness, and after that also King of Salem, which is, King of peace" (Heb. 7:2).

So we see that a tithe was given unto God, not out of compulsion, but because of the love these two patriarchs had for God. It was after the law was given at Sinai that God became specific as to what was to be given and how much as we see in Leviticus 27:32.

> And concerning the tithe of the herd, or of the flock, even of whatsoever passeth under the rod, the tenth shall be holy unto the LORD. (Leviticus 27:32)

Tithing is not commanded under the laws of the New Testament concerning the church; yet, we give because we love God and want to see the Gospel spread throughout the whole world. If we give ten percent and stop there while possessing the ability to give more, then we have not grasped the dynamic and blessing-filled principle of giving.

B. Storehouse

When we look at the storehouse, we see that this is referring to the temple which was the center of worship for Israel. Since there is no more central temple worship akin to that of ancient Israel, we must search the Bible and ask what our temple is, and then we will find out what our storehouse is. We read the following:

> Know ye not that ye are the temple of God, and that the Spirit of God dwelleth in you? (1 Corinthians 3:16)

> And what agreement hath the temple of God with idols? for ye are the temple of the living God; as God hath said, I will dwell in them, and walk in them; and I will be their God, and they shall be my people. (2 Corinthians 6:16)

> In whom all the building fitly framed together groweth unto an holy temple in the Lord. (Ephesians 2:21)

We see clearly that the temple in the New Testament refers to the body of Christ, namely the Church. Therefore, God is telling us that the church is the storehouse in which we bring our tithes and offerings. Now does this mean the organized local church is the only storehouse? The answer is no, because suppose you belong to a church which does not have a missions program, and the offerings only go to upkeep of the facilities and pay salaries. If you sent part of your offering to a mission's organization or a godly radio ministry, then in essence, you are bringing the offerings into the storehouse, which is the body of Christ. My personal belief is that a church without a missions program is a church without purpose.

C. Test Me

> Bring ye all the tithes into the storehouse, that there may be meat in mine house, and prove me now herewith, saith the LORD of hosts, if I will not open you the windows of heaven, and pour you out a blessing, that there shall not be room enough to receive it. (Malachi 3:10)

We must be careful here that we do not misunderstand what these words are teaching. God is not telling us to look at heaven and, with an unholy boldness, challenge him. Instead, he is giving us a gentle nudge and saying that he wants us to see his faithfulness. God is telling us that if we have enough faith to give to his true work, then we can ask him to show us how faithful he is. This is the only place in Scripture where the Lord tells us to prove him, and he would not put that in the Bible if he did not want us to.

Here is my personal experience with this verse when it was explained to me about giving. I had just become a Christian and believed that if I did not give massive amounts of money to God's work, then he would do bad things to me because I would be disobedient. I was living in Hackettstown, New Jersey, at the time, and I was making a small salary; yet, I was giving way beyond my means and was carrying much debt with 19–21 percent interest rates. My view of God was erroneous. After I told the man who discipled me that I was in strapping debt and giving above my means, he pointed me to the above verse. He counseled me to get out of debt. He said, "The Lord doesn't want you living with all that debt."

I then bowed my head and prayed the verse back to God and "tested him." If I remember correctly, it was within two weeks that I received over $750. When I did not give for a while till I saw my debt reduced and finally coming out of debtor's prison, my friend said to me, "See, the Lord didn't throw a lightning bolt at you, did he?"

I believe God wants us to have stability in our finances, and when we include God in that budget, he will stabilize them. However, keep in mind there will be times of testing, and that does not mean God is not keeping his word. He is either preparing you or correcting you for something. Giving to God's work does not guarantee you will become wealthy either. Just give and leave the blessings to God.

The Way You Give Is the Way You Will Receive!

"Give, and it shall be given unto you; good measure, pressed down, and shaken together, and running over, shall men give into your bosom. For with the same measure that ye mete withal it shall be measured to you again" (Luke 6:38).

Let me give an incident concerning a friend of mine. I remember showing a movie called *God's of the New Age* at my home church where I had just preached the morning message. I put a plate on the table by the refreshments and placed a little message above the plate that all money collected would go to World Missionary Press for tracts to India. My friend dug deep in his pockets and gave eighty-five cents.

If you are cheap with God, he will be cheap with you. Keep in mind, it is not the size of the gift that counts but the attitude. If we give a small amount with an abundant attitude, God will bless accordingly at his discretion. Cheap Christians are not happy Christians. Poor Christians who can only give one dollar joyfully will be blessed above and beyond the cheap Christian who grudgingly gives $10.

I believe that when we are cheap and grudgingly throw our money in the plate with the wrong attitude, the money becomes invisible to the eyes of God (he who has ears to hear).

We Will Reap What We Sow

"Be not deceived; God is not mocked: for whatsoever a man soweth, that shall he also reap" (Galatians 6:7).

This verse is a general principle verse, but I include it because it also applies to finances. If you sow little, you will reap little. If you sow abundantly, you will reap abundantly. If you plant ten stalks of corn, you may get fifty ears, but if you plant 100 stalks, you may get 500 ears. You will reap what you sow and without crop failure. If you sow cheap, others will be cheap with you and to a greater extent. If you sow in abundance, others will be generous with you. The principle works.

No Tax-Deductible Receipt?

Sometimes there are personal ministries, whether on the Internet or in person, where the person or persons have not set up a nonprofit status. Perhaps the ministry is small and may remain that way. If that person begins to struggle and they ask for help, how will you respond? Will you give if you do not receive a tax-deductible receipt? If you refuse to give because you want that receipt, then you must check your motives for giving.

The IRS is not your benefactor. If a small ministry is faithfully sending out the gospel and you refuse to give unless you get a receipt, then you are showing your trust is in the IRS and not God! God's principles for giving are not negated by the fact that a receipt is not issued. God can bless much more than the IRS. Tax deductible receipts have been used of Satan to stop many believers from giving to the Lord's work under the guise of "proper stewardship." This is false stewardship, because the work of the Lord will be hindered unless a receipt is issued.

I think it is interesting that we spend hundreds, even thousands of dollars a year, on junk for the house, the lawn, the car, etc.; but when a decision has to be made to give a few dollars to a Christian ministry that does not or cannot give receipts, then we close the wallet and say, "Well, we want to be able to deduct our contributions, because that is wise stewardship." Then in the same breath, they are on the run to the nearest Walmart to buy more personal junk which will be sold at their yard sale in one year.

Is that wise stewardship? Christians should not be concerned as to whether they receive a receipt or not; they should be concerned about their faithfulness to the Lord in sending out the Gospel.

Six Basic Dynamics Which Giving Builds into Our Lives:

1. It teaches us to look beyond ourselves as we see the needs of others.
2. It teaches us we are stewards and not owners.
3. It arrests greed and self-centeredness.
4. It opens the door for a sacrificial life.
5. It teaches us that we can trust God with money which opens the door to trust him with other things.
6. Obedience.

How to Detect a False Gospel

If there is one thing which is going to characterize these last days we are living in, it is the flourishing of the false gospels. I wanted to include a section with some hints to help you identify a false gospel. Keep in mind that not all false gospels are cults like the Mormons or Roman Catholics, but they are found in many Protestant churches. This not only includes small out-of-the-way churches but those of mainline denominations. Sometimes identifying a false gospel can be difficult, but those that hold to false gospels will eventually expose themselves. Let us look at some of the teachings which will help us identify the false so you may be on guard.

Jesus Christ

If he is thought of as only a prophet, teacher, holy man, martyr, sect leader, and is not taught that he is God, then you have entered into a false gospel. Run for your spiritual life. If they doubt his resurrection, ascension, and miracles on earth, then they are a false gospel.

The Holy Spirit

If he is spoken of as a force or power. He is the third person of the Godhead and coequal with God the Father and God the Son. If they speak of him as an impersonal force or anything less than God, then you have stepped into a false gospel.

The Bible

How does your group or church view the Bible? Are they saying we don't have an infallible Bible today? Have they replaced the King James Bible with modern translations and then vehemently denigrate the King James Bible? Does the pastor or leader continually tell you that certain verses should not be in the Bible? Do they doubt parts of the Bible such as denying the teachings of the miracles? Do they deny the existence of Satan and angels? Any attack upon the Scriptures will give you an insight into the unsaved state of the preacher or teacher. Do they deny the inerrancy of Scripture?

Signs, Wonders, and Tongues

If the church or group you visit believes in things like speaking in tongues, slain in the Spirit, prosperity, healing, visions, verbal prophecies, and rock music instead of music glorifying God, then you have stepped into a false gospel. The Charismatic/Pentecostal movement is the binding cord of ecumenicalism.

Roman Catholic Sympathizing

If you go to a church or group which is sympathetic to Roman Catholicism, then you have entered a false gospel. Roman Catholicism is a descendant of the religions of Egypt and Babylon and has nothing to do with the true gospel.

Free Will and Loss of Salvation

If you find a group which teaches that you can lose your salvation or believes that you can "accept Christ," then you have wandered into a false gospel. Man does not have free will as we are either slaves of Satan or servants of Christ (Romans 6:17–18).

As you progress in the Christian faith, you will find many more ways the church has become the enemy of Christ. If you cannot find a good church or a home group, then it is spiritually safer that you stay home and start your own group. I can guarantee there will be a small group of like-minded believers who will have the same disdain for the false teachings. Eventually, all the true Christians will probably go back to house churches anyway, which is the New Testament model for the weekly meeting of Christians.

Keys to Finding Your Spiritual Gifts

Probably one of the most confusing things in all of Christendom is the identifying and application of one's spiritual gifts. This subject is tackled in many ways, but I wish to bring to light some major characteristics which accompany the spiritual gifts. This is by no means an exhaustive listing, but it will serve its purpose by helping a Christian identify in their own life some traits which synchronize with the spiritual gifts. In this manner, a believer will then be able to establish reasons for their peculiar actions which may have seemed unusual without a cause. Once a connection is made between behavior and thought patterns with traits of a spiritual gift, then this person is on their way to discovering their spiritual gift and finding their proper place in the service of God.

    In this section, I wish to classify the three sets of spiritual gifts which God gives us in the Scriptures, and then I will make an attempt to distinguish each set of gifts. I was saved for about five years before I discovered my spiritual gifts. My two gifts are teaching and exhortation. I discovered my gift of teaching by reason of the fact that I do not mind being chained to a desk for long hours and receive much satisfaction when others profit from my studies. I found I love to teach Bible studies and just open the Word to believers, plus God has given me a good understanding of Scripture through these studies.

    When I discovered these things, I realized there had to be a reason for it. When I began a study of the gifts, God opened my eyes to the fact I had the gift of teaching. The discovery of my gift of exhortation came out of my method of teaching God's principles to the saints. I had begun to write studies which were biblically based and which consistently carried the expression of encouragement and motivation of the believer.

This is my personal testimony of how I discovered my spiritual gifts, and I will be bold to say that you too will find this an efficient way to identify your spiritual gifts. I deeply believe that your actions are directly related to your spiritual gifts. Your actions and your attitudes are the key to finding your spiritual gifts. This will become apparent as you ponder the outward actions of the model people which I believe represent the gifts that we will discuss. May God guide you and build you up as you seek his place for your ministry.

The Provisional Gifts

The provisional gifts are found in 1 Corinthians 12:8–11:

> For to one is given by the Spirit the word of wisdom; to another the word of knowledge by the same Spirit; {9} To another faith by the same Spirit; to another the gifts of healing by the same Spirit; {10} To another the working of miracles; to another prophecy; to another discerning of spirits; to another divers kinds of tongues; to another the interpretation of tongues: {11} But all these worketh that one and the selfsame Spirit, dividing to every man severally as he will. (1 Corinthians 12:8–11)

These gifts are also commonly called "the sign gifts," which were exclusive to the church in its embryonic stage. These gifts were definitely temporary. When the Bible was completed, six of these temporary gifts were transferred to all believers throughout history and will be till the last day. Three of them ceased when the completion of the Bible occurred. These three will be the first ones we will examine.

Tongues—A language, especially a learned one. This gift was given when the Bible was nearing completion, and God was still giving direct messages to the church via the spoken word. It was used to bring God's message to those of different languages as plainly seen in Acts 2:4–12.

Interpretation of Tongues—This gift was required in the church of Corinth, because their gift of tongues was different from those of Acts. The tongues of Corinth were a phenomenon which required an interpreter for the church. The tongues in Acts were established languages (Acts 2:6). The tongues of Corinth also carried messages from God.

Prophecy—This gift was one which also received messages from God and relayed them to the people akin to the prophets of old. These people were to declare God's Word to the church. These messages were verbal in nature.

As you can plainly, see these three gifts were involved with receiving messages from God on a verbal note. Since the Bible was completed, we no longer have any need for new divine communication since God has told us in Revelation 22:18–19 that he will no longer communicate with us verbally but will communicate with us by means of his Word, the completed Bible. These legitimate gifts ceased because there were no longer a need for them.

> For I testify unto every man that heareth the words of the prophecy of this book, If any man shall add unto these things, God shall add unto him the plagues that are written in this book: {19} And if any man shall take away from the words of the book of this prophecy, God shall take away his part out of the book of life, and out of the holy city, and from the things which are written in this book. (Revelation 22:18–19)

The second part of the provisional gifts are the ones which were made available to every Christian since the completion of the Bible. I will list them and give scriptural reference for each one.

Wisdom

"If any of you lack wisdom, let him ask of God, that giveth to all men liberally, and upbraideth not; and it shall be given him" (James 1:5).

No longer is wisdom a gift to be enjoyed by a few, but it is available to every believer as the verse teaches us.

Knowledge

"But grow in grace, and in the knowledge of our Lord and Saviour Jesus Christ. To him be glory both now and forever. Amen" (2 Peter 3:18).

Here is a good example that the gift of knowledge has become universal in the body of Christ. With the completion of the Bible, we can come to a knowledge of Christ and God without a special spiritual gift.

Faith

"For therein is the righteousness of God revealed from faith to faith: as it is written, The just shall live by faith" (Romans 1:17).

Who are the just? The just are every born-again believer. With that in mind, we see the gift of faith is no longer needed since every child of God is to live by faith. Nowhere except in the early church does God call this a gift. After the completion of the Bible, he expects every believer to exercise faith, and we are not to refer to those people with great faith as having the gift of faith, because this is not biblical. Faith is a fruit of the Holy Spirit and given to every true believer.

> But the fruit of the Spirit is love, joy, peace, longsuffering, gentleness, goodness, faith, (Galatians 5:22)

Discerning Spirits

"Beloved, believe not every spirit, but try the spirits whether they are of God: because many false prophets are gone out into the world" (1 John 4:1).

No longer must we seek out the gift of discerning of spirits to help us determine if a doctrine is false. With the completion of the Bible, we have all that is needed to verify a doctrinal teaching.

Miracles

"But ye shall receive power, after that the Holy Ghost is come upon you: and ye shall be witnesses unto me both in Jerusalem, and in all Judaea, and in Samaria, and unto the uttermost part of the earth" (Acts 1:8).

The word *miracle* in 1 Corinthians 12:10 is the Greek word *dunamis*, which means "power, force, or ability." This word has nothing to do with miracles as we know them today. For example, a miracle would be an instantaneous replacement of a lost limb or a withered hand which is made whole or someone raised from the dead. If you would take a concordance, you would see that this word is specifically used in the context of spreading the gospel. The miracle worked today is the miracle of salvation. This gift is also universal in the body of Christ since every born-again Christian is endued with the power of God, the Holy Spirit.

Healing

"Who his own self bare our sins in his own body on the tree, that we, being dead to sins, should live unto righteousness: by whose stripes ye were healed" (1 Peter 2:24).

Before the completion of the Scriptures, God used the healing of the sick to show visually what salvation is like. The sick person represented a sinful person, and the healed person represented a saved person. God used physical healing for the sole purpose of showing the difference between the saved and the unsaved. Every healing was a visual parable, the earthly story with the heavenly meaning.

There is no doubt in my mind that Jesus can heal today, but it is in response to two methods:

The Will of God—Many times, we see unbelievers who were healed of a deadly disease. Now the unbeliever chalks it up to luck or modern medicine, but they never give God the credit, even though they might give God or "the Man upstairs" a passing thought.

Fervent Prayer—Many times, God will allow sickness in a family or church to arouse an apathetic group. He may heal in response to the sincere prayers of his people. I know of a woman who was cured of terminal cancer by God in response to the prayers of an entire church.

The type of healing that is with us today is spiritual healing. This is why in James 5, we are exhorted to send for the elders of the church. If we are physically sick, then we see a medical doctor or nutritionist; but when it comes to spiritual affairs, we invoke the elders of the church for prayer and counsel.

Galatians 6:1 tells us that we are to restore a believer who is caught up in sin. This is the type of healing God has in view for the believer. For the unbeliever, the healing God has in view is becoming saved. God is more interested in healing our spiritual sickness than our physical sickness, which he does with great joy if it is his will to do so.

Spiritual healing focuses on eternity's values, while physical healing focuses on temporal values. Out of these two, which one is important? Whenever a believer opens the Word of God and begins to declare it to someone, they are in essence initiating spiritual healing in that person's life. This is the type of healing we Christians shall partake of and pursue, not physical healing.

Miraculous physical healing was never part of God's great commission. We are to teach all nations, not physically heal all nations. With biblical references, we have concluded that the provisional gifts were turned into universal gifts in the body of Christ, except for three of them which were discontinued by the end of the first century.

The Office Gifts

The next set of gifts we need to decipher is known as the "Office Gifts." These are found in Ephesians 4:11–12. The office gifts were given for the purpose of the assignment of individual ministries which in the aggregate would constitute the church universal in its optimum mode of existence. Each Christian is given a spiritual gift which, when combined with the gifts of others, would allow a local assembly of believers to be fully equipped to fulfill the mandate of the Great Commission. Every Christian has at least one of the office gifts. The office gifts are specific ministries with specific tasks attached to each one.

Apostles—"one who is sent"

The apostles of the early church were those who received messages directly from Christ and who saw him. They were the catalysts of the local churches. They were eyewitnesses to the miracles and/or teachings of Christ.

> Even as they delivered them unto us, which from the beginning were eyewitnesses, and ministers of the word; (Luke 1:2)

> Truly the signs of an apostle were wrought among you in all patience, in signs, and wonders, and mighty deeds. (2 Corinthians 12:12)

As the church began to expand, the word *apostle* began to take on a wider meaning and began to include those who were not eyewitnesses but were considered testimonies of the gospel of Christ. Barnabas was considered to be an apostle.

> Which when the apostles, Barnabas and Paul, heard of, they rent their clothes, and ran in among the people, crying out, (Acts 14:14)

There is no biblical evidence that he ever saw the Lord with his eyes. So as we see in Scripture, the term was widened in its usage to the point that all believers are, in essence, apostles, because we are sent. The Great Commission is our marching orders. We do not receive any new revelation, but we use the Scriptures as our source of truth, plus every believer is a testimony to the grace of God.

Prophets—"One who declares God's Word"

I believe this gift has remained unchanged from the early church. The prophet was and is the person who declares God's Word, which means his entire life and mind are programmed to Scripture. He is the spiritual shop steward who raises the flag every time an incorrect doctrine is taught. He keeps the local assembly and the leaders biblically correct. His points of contention may seem petty, but it must be remembered that a huge tree grows out of a small seed. So it is with false doctrines. All it needs is a foot in the door, and it will begin to mushroom uncontrollably. If you think it cannot happen in your church, look around to the major denominations that were bastions of truth just fifty years ago.

Evangelists—"Bringer of Good News"

This person has the ability to speak to large groups of people. They speak mainly on the redemptive part of the Gospel. The evangelist is concerned with dispensing the Gospel to as many people as possible. They view the spread of the Gospel as their only reason of existence. They possess a burning desire in their souls to tell of the salvation God gives to man. Now in the smaller sense of the word, each believer is an evangelist. Each time you give a tract to someone or verbally witness, you are bringing the good news. You do it on a smaller scale, and the evangelist does it on a larger scale.

Pastors—"Shepherds"

The pastor is normally the head of a local assembly, having oversight of the flock. He is the spiritual leader and cares for all his people on an equal basis. He is there to encourage, counsel, motivate, and discipline. There is a little "pastor" in each of us as we minister to others or disciple them; we are being a shepherd to them. A Godly pastor will show very good leadership ability. Those with dictatorial attitudes do not possess the gift of a pastor.

Teachers—"An Instructor"

The teacher is the person who lives to dispense information. The teacher takes the Word of God and doles out information from it in a systematic way which will both inform and build up the Christian. The teacher's gift is so intense they teach whether they are in an official or unofficial capacity. A teacher will be unable to stay in a church where they are not permitted or encouraged to exercise their gift. This is not pride but is the gift which God has placed within them for teaching and helping others to understand the Bible. The teacher also filters information to determine if certain teachings are true.[3]

The Preparation Gifts

These gifts are most important, because it is through these we determine what our ministry is and where we are best suited to serve.

---

[3] NOTE: Many pastors claim the title "Pastor-Teacher" which they believe is one gift and not two. I have sought many Greek references and have not found these words to be one. The two words are always found with *kai* between them which is translated "and." It separates two distinct words. In verse 11–13, the word *tous* which translates "the" is found before each of the gifts listed, except teachers. It seems that pastors and teachers are two distinct gifts. One reason I believe this is there are many gifted women teachers out there yet God forbids them to be pastors. If it is one gift, then the women must become pastors to teach, which would violate God's word. A pastor may have the gift of teaching, which would coincide beautifully with his office of pastor.

These seven gifts prepare us for the office gifts. They may also help us determine our vocation. They are found in Romans 12:6–8.

> Having then gifts differing according to the grace that is given to us, whether prophecy, let us prophesy according to the proportion of faith; {7} Or ministry, let us wait on our ministering: or he that teacheth, on teaching; {8} Or he that exhorteth, on exhortation: he that giveth, let him do it with simplicity; he that ruleth, with diligence; he that showeth mercy, with cheerfulness. (Romans 12:6–8)

I now offer the following traits, which I believe will help you identify your spiritual gift(s) so you may begin to develop it, and then you will find your proper place of service.

Prophecy

Definition: To speak forth, prophetic declarations, exhortations and warnings
Characteristics: Elijah
Scripture: 1 Kings 18
Vs. 1—They are programmed to Scripture because they are motivated by Scripture. They are normally heard asking the question, "Where do you read that in the Bible?"
Vs. 18—Have a note of warning in their speech.
Vs. 18—They will normally point out specific sins.
Vs. 19—They normally will have a confrontational spirit.
Vs. 19—They normally emphasize the judgment of God.
Vs. 21—They offer black and white solutions.
Vs. 22—They sometimes believe they are alone when it comes to understanding truth.
Vs. 27—They seem to have an uncaring or caustic personality.
Vv. 37–39—They usually bring people back to the Lord by fear.
Vs. 46—There is always a sense of urgency in their life.

Ministry

Definition: Service, Servant, or Attendance
Characteristics: Timothy
Scripture: Selected
Acts 17:15—A desire to serve others.
Acts 19:21–22—They are happy to follow orders and be support personnel.
1 Corinthians 4:17—They are faithful servants.
1 Corinthians 16:10—They have an inner joy serving others.
Philippians 2:20—They are fulfilled while serving others.
Philippians 2:21–22—They look for opportunities to serve others.
1 Thessalonians 3:6—They serve without complaining.
1 Timothy 1:2—They are happy to be disciples.
1 Timothy 1:18–20—They do not fear hindrances to God's work but view them as opportunities.
Philemon 1—The servant identifies with the teacher, master, or project at hand.

Exhortation

Definition: Comfort, Entreat, To call to one, Call near, or Call for.
Characteristics: Paul
Scripture: Selected
Romans 6:6–7 and 11–13—The exhorter desires to give precise steps of action in stimulating a believer to growth.
1 Corinthians 1:10—The Exhorter takes a person at the point of where they are and encourages them to grow.
2 Corinthians 7:3—The Exhorter does not condemn but makes no excuse for sin either.
Galatians 3:1—The Exhorter counsels on a personal basis and avoids programmed procedures.
Philippians 1:12—The Exhorter sees tribulation as a method of spiritual growth.
Colossians 1:9–12—The Exhorter desires to see the Christian reach their maximum spiritual potential.

Colossians 1:28—The Exhorter sees the full potential of every believer.
1 Thessalonians 2:8–9—The Exhorter stays with someone until they are restored.

Giving

Definition: Share or Impart
Characteristics: Matthew
Scripture: Book of Matthew
Matthew must have had the gift of giving since he penned many principles of handling money in the book named after him. Tithing does not mean you have the gift of giving!
5:42—The giver has inward joy giving to those who have need.
5:46–47—The giver does not expect nor require a pay back.
6:1–4—The giver desires to give in secret.
6:19–20—The giver has the ability to make wise investments.
6:24—The giver views money as a vehicle not a goal.
6:25—The giver is satisfied with the basic necessities of life.
7:6—The giver is very cautious where they invest their money.
10:8—The giver sees the money in their possession as God's and he has the right to claim it for his needs.
10:9—The giver is frugal.
10:38—Sacrificial giving is a way of life for the Giver.
13:46—The giver has the ability to make wise purchases.
16:26—The giver does not have an inward desire to stash away the Lord's money in worldly investments. If they do, it is in short term investments for easier access and no penalties.
18:8–9—The Giver may rebuke a cheap Christian.

Ruling

Definition: Preside or Set Over
Characteristics: Solomon
Scripture: Selected

1 Kings 3:8–9—The Ruler sees himself as a servant with no self-ambitions.
1 Kings 3:23–28—The Ruler is able to make wise and discerning judgments.
1 Kings 4:1–19—The Ruler has the ability to delegate authority.
1 Kings 5:5—The Ruler can see the big picture and results of a major project.
1 Kings 5:6, 13—The Ruler can see what is needed to complete the task at hand.
1 Kings 5:8, 12—The Ruler can deal rightly with other leaders.
1 Kings 5:14—The Ruler has the ability to assign the right people to the right tasks.
1 Kings 6:38–7:1—The Ruler has the desire to tackle and accomplish many tasks.
2 Chronicles 2:9—The Ruler is a planner and a schedule keeper.
2 Chronicles 7:4–5—The Ruler identifies himself with his people in a given task.
Proverbs 22:13—The Ruler abhors excuses by lazy people.

Mercy

Definition: To have the desire of relieving the miserable or to have pity upon by actually relieving them.
Characteristics: Apostle John
Scripture: The Gospel of John
John must have had the gift of mercy as he wrote much about merciful acts, plus he was the disciple whom Jesus trusted to care for his earthly mother. It is interesting to note that Jesus had earthly brothers and sisters, yet John was given the task to care for Mary.
3:30—Mercy puts the needs of others before their own needs.
4:9—Mercy does not care if the person that needs help is an enemy.
4:14—Mercy understands the deeper needs of others.
5:6—Mercy will attach themselves to the poor and helpless, in both material and spiritual areas.

5:8–9—Mercy will remain with a person until healing or improvement happens.
6:15—Mercy tends to shy away from public ministry or life.
6:26—Mercy may become a mark for their sympathetic virtues.
7:3–4—Mercy may be misunderstood that they are seeking notoriety.
9:2–3,6–7—Mercy is more concerned about healing than cause.
11:35—Mercy identifies with the sorrow someone is feeling.
11:36—Mercy builds deeper friendships than normal.
18:10–11—Mercy may rebuke people who cause pain.

<u>Teaching</u>

Definition: Instruction or Instructor
Characteristics: Luke
Scripture: Luke 1:1–4

1. (*Many have taken in hand*)—A teacher holds back information until all pertinent material is in.
2. A teacher is careful of their information sources (Entire verse).
3. (*It seemed good to me*)—A teacher has an attitude of joy in doing research.

    (*to me also*)—A teacher realizes he is part of the body of Christ and does not hold sole interpretation.

    (*perfect understanding*)—A teacher will have optimum understanding of the material ("perfect" denotes follow closely, trace, examine). The teacher does not accept another's teaching unless it completely harmonizes in the entire Bible.

    (*of all things*)—A teacher is concerned with all facts and details.

    (*to write*)—A teacher is happy to be chained to a desk for many hours.

    (*unto thee*)—A teacher personalizes the Scriptures for daily living.

(*in order*)—"Order" means in succession or consecutive order. The teacher has the desire to deliver truth in a systematic way.
4. (*that thou mightest know*)—The teacher is concerned that their hearers understand.

(*the certainty of those things*)—The teacher teaches with absolutes. "Certainty" means firmness, steadfastness, stability.

(*wherein thou hast been instructed*)—The teacher takes previously written material, tests it by Scripture and either clarifies it or rejects it.

The Importance of Knowing Our Spiritual Gift(s)!

"I don't even know if I have a spiritual gift" is the cry of many Christians. I have heard this statement from different Christians. The ones I heard it from are spiritually frustrated and do not seem to fit in anywhere. The results of this situation are you become a destabilizing element to those who know and are attempting to develop their spiritual gifts. There are two very important reasons why Christians need to know their spiritual gift.

So You May Work Where God Has Qualified You

Have you ever called a plumber to wire up a house or called a carpenter to do arthroscopic surgery? Of course not. While these people are all qualified to do a certain job, they are not qualified to do the wrong job. The same principle applies to the spiritual realm. God has given different gifts to different Christians, because there are different ministries within the body of Christ. Picture this scenario within a local church: All givers but no teachers—this would result in a rich but spiritually illiterate church. All servants but no leaders would result in "everyone doing what was right in their own eyes," and there would be chaos in the structure of the church.

Have you ever seen a zombie in a Sci-fi movie? This is how a Christian moves without knowing their spiritual gifts. We are spiritual zombies, because we have no direction in our lives, owing to the fact we do not know what direction to go in. As soon as a believer discovers their spiritual gift, they immediately begin the task of developing that gift, and instantly, direction will begin to appear.

This direction will lead to a ministry you will feel comfortable with. The reason you will feel comfortable is that you are now developing the gift which God has placed within you. Spiritual frustration develops when a Christian attempts to develop a gift they do not have or wish they had. Their Christian walk will be one of frustration and envy when they see God using others instead of them.

God Has a Ministry for Every Believer

God did not save any Christian for the purpose of coming to church to listen to a sermon and then go home and wait till next week to hear another sermon. Many believers suffer frustration because they see no reason of existence. This is normally verbalized by the statement, "Why did God save me?" Believers will stagnate unless they seek that reason of existence. God has a plan for every believer to be utilized in the Great Commission, whether home or abroad.

One reason many Christians are frustrated is they have relegated ministry to the church leaders. They inwardly believe there is such a thing as the "chosen chosen;" in other words, those with gifted abilities and those without. This is nowhere found in the Bible. This is why we have much pastoral burnout and many Christians with excessive leisure time. One group is overcommitted, and the other group is under committed. If every Christian would find and develop their spiritual gift, the Christian church would not be on the run from every cult, anti-Christian judge, or political pressure group. The church would be mighty as God intended it to be.

He gave the gifts for us to be empowered. If you choose to be idle, then you may expect defeat in your walk, but if you live in power, according to your spiritual gifts, then you may suffer setbacks, but never overwhelming defeat. God requires faithfulness in a steward, and we are all stewards of the spiritual gifts he has given us.

> Moreover it is required in stewards, that a man be found faithful. (1 Corinthians 4:2)

The time for idle living is over, because it is almost too late.

Finding God's Will

Let us look at the mystery of the ages which is the will of God. The will of God has plagued Christians down through the ages since there seems to be much mystery surrounding it. Many Christians go from coast to coast, trying to find God's will for their life.

Is it really a mystery? Must we go from cradle to grave, trying to seek God's will for our lives? I believe the Bible has given clear direction regarding God's will for our lives. We get into trouble when we take our desires and try to make them God's will for our lives. In essence, we impose our desired will on our lived and completely overlook God's will. If we take the following Scriptures, we will see some specific principles which will help uncover the will of God.

The word *will* in the following verses may also be translated, "choice, determination," but specifically "purpose." If we take the word *purpose* and place it next to *will*, we will gain further understanding of these verses.

> Paul, called to be an apostle of Jesus Christ through the will [purpose] of God, and Sosthenes our brother. (1 Corinthians 1:1)

Paul was called an apostle for the purpose of God. Let's pose the question, what was God's purpose for Paul? God's purpose for Paul was to start churches in various parts of Asia and help sustain them, plus write a portion of the New Testament under the inspiration of the Holy Spirit.

> Wherefore be ye not unwise, but understanding what the will [*purpose*] of the Lord is. (Ephesians 5:17)

This verse seems to be the pivotal verse in this entire chapter since it warns us to walk properly in the faith and that we must no longer identify with the ways of the world. This verse is a warning to us that we must understand that the will of God is to walk circumspectly.

> Not with eyeservice, as men pleasers; but as the servants of Christ, doing the will [purpose] of God from the heart; (Ephesians 6:6)

This verse states that we should do God's work with a true heart and not to impress others. The purpose of God for every believer is a heartfelt service for him.

> For this is the will [*purpose*] of God, even your sanctification, that ye should abstain from fornication: (1 Thessalonians 4:3)

This verse states the will of God is possessive sanctification. We are already sanctified in position because of our salvation, but Paul is telling us to possess our sanctification. This means that we have been set apart by God for God and we must live the separated life in both body and mind.

> In everything give thanks: for this is the will [*purpose*] of God in Christ Jesus concerning you. (1 Thessalonians 5:18)

This verse tells us the believer is to be thankful in all things. This thanksgiving must be from the heart and not the lips.

> And the world passeth away, and the lust thereof: but he that doeth the will [*purpose*] of God abideth forever. (1 John 2:17)

This verse tells us the believer is to walk in the purpose of God, which is obedience. This is a "proof of salvation" verse, because John is telling us that if someone does God's will, they will abide forever. This is not referring to works which some believe lead to salvation but is speaking of doing the will of God as a result of salvation. We are the testimonies to an evil world as we walk according to God's word. Our works are the manifestation of our salvation.

In these six verses, we have seen the will (*purpose*) of every believer is to live a holy and obedient life. This is the first prerequisite for discovering the will of God for your life. Sin hinders our relationship with God. When a Christian sins, they block out God's voice of guidance which is not an audible voice. If you are living in sin, do not expect God to communicate his will for your life, because he cannot reach you due to sin interference. I wish to turn to a specific purpose which God has given to every believer.

> Go ye therefore, and teach all nations, baptizing them in the name of the Father, and of the Son, and of the Holy Ghost: {20} Teaching them to observe all things whatsoever I have commanded you: and, lo, I am with you always, even unto the end of the world. Amen. (Matthew 28:19–20)

The second purpose a believer has is to spread the gospel to the entire world. Each believer has a part in this, and God holds cheap and lazy Christians accountable for their nonparticipation in this command. I fail to understand why some Christians believe they are exempt from this command while others must foot the bills for their noncompliance. If Christians would tithe and stop screaming legalism, God's program of world evangelism would be well-funded.

Why is it when we want to do something nice for ourselves, we are under grace; but as soon as the preacher mentions tithing, suddenly we call it law and throw up our theological arguments? The second prerequisite for finding the personal will of God in our lives is the desire to do our part in the Great Commission.

The third area God gives us to find his personal will in our lives is spiritual gifts. Each of us must discover which spiritual gift(s) we possess so we may begin to search out our proper place of service. For example, the gift of mercy would not make a good ruler nor the gift of prophecy a good counselor. God has given spiritual gifts with certain parameters. The third prerequisite for finding the will of God is knowing your spiritual gift. This is a must if a Christian is to find their proper sphere of service.

The reasons so many Christians feel out of place in their present sphere of service is that they have a spiritual gift which differs from the job they are doing. A quick analogy would be that you would not call a plumber to hook up electricity. Many times, believers work outside the parameters because help is hard to find, so we wear many hats. We have heard it said that 10 percent of the people do 90 percent of the work. Many Christians view Christianity as a spectator sport, and as a result, others have to do twice the amount of work. This results in many Christians doing jobs they are not spiritually empowered to do. In the last chapter, we saw how we could discover our spiritual gifts.

The fourth area which God gives us to find his will for our life is our talents. Has God given you the ability to sing, write, preach, organize, fix things, make things, cook, bake, handle children, handle senior citizens, teach, listen, etc.? What is your talent or talents? List what you believe are your talents, and don't neglect the obvious ones. Finding your talents will help you determine where you can serve God best. The fourth prerequisite for finding the personal will of God is knowing your talents.

Let's list the prerequisites:

1. A holy and obedient life.
2. The desire to send forth the gospel.
3. The knowledge of your spiritual gift(s).
4. The knowledge of your talents.

A person who has the gift of teaching and the ability to sing may sing Christian songs with lyrics that teach truth from the Bible.

A person who has the gift of ruling and can bake may open a bakery with the purpose of supporting Christian missions.

A person with the gift of mercy and the talent to cook may invite a poor person to their home for a meal and a witness. They may volunteer at a rescue mission or soup kitchen.

The combination of spiritual gifts and talents are limited only by the creativity of the Creator. The will of God is wherever God has placed you at this moment with the spiritual gifts you possess and the talents you possess as you are presently using them. If you believe God wants you to make a move, do your research, because there are many voices out there, and they are all not of God. Satan loves to confuse the believer and does a good job of it unless we stay spiritually astute.

If God wants you to move, he will initiate the procedure. Have you ever been laid off from a job? This is one method God uses to initiate a move in a person's life. Many times, Christians will run ahead of God, and this is where confusion enters in. If God begins to put a move into your heart, then at that point, begin to prepare yourself for the time when God will finalize your move.

The keyword is *prepare,* just as the Israelites prepared to move when the pillar of fire or cloud moved (Numbers 9:21). If you prepare, the transition will be less traumatic. God's will for your life is not a mystery if we just enact the four prerequisites listed.

God does not want his will for us to be a mystery, because if he did, how would we get the gospel out? God has made it plain and simple for us—all we need do is apply the principles. Let me inject the fact that sometimes God makes us wait for his timing. If you are convinced God wants you to do something, just because he makes you wait does not mean you are out of the will of God.

God has a purpose for every single believer, no matter who they are or what their social status is. Do not let the term "God's Will" frighten you, because as his child, he has promised you guidance and wisdom for your life.

> Thou shalt guide me with thy counsel, and afterward receive me to glory. (Psalm 73:24)

> If any of you lack wisdom, let him ask of God, that giveth to all men liberally, and upbraideth not; and it shall be given him. (James 1:5)

> For whosoever shall do the will of God, the same is my brother, and my sister, and mother. (Mark 3:35)

> For David, after he had served his own generation by the will of God, fell on sleep, and was laid unto his fathers, and saw corruption: (Acts 13:36)

> Making request, if by any means now at length I might have a prosperous journey by the will of God to come unto you. (Romans 1:10)

> And he that searcheth the hearts knoweth what is the mind of the Spirit, because he maketh intercession for the saints according to the will of God. (Romans 8:27)

> And be not conformed to this world: but be ye transformed by the renewing of your mind, that ye may prove what is that good, and acceptable, and perfect, will of God. (Romans 12:2)

That I may come unto you with joy by the will of God, and may with you be refreshed. (Romans 15:32)

Paul, an apostle of Jesus Christ by the will of God, and Timothy our brother, unto the church of God which is at Corinth, with all the saints which are in all Achaia: (2 Corinthians 1:1)

Man

The word for *man* in the Greek, in which the New Testament was written, is *anthropos,* which is the general term for man which includes both females and males. There are other words in the Greek which specify male or female. You can see that we get the word *anthropology* from *anthropos*. The word for *man* in the Hebrew, in which the Old Testament was written, is *awdawm*, which is also the generic term for man. There are specific words in the Hebrew for male and female.

Created in the Image of God

"And God said, 'Let us make man in our image, after our likeness: and let them have dominion over the fish of the sea, and over the fowl of the air, and over the cattle, and over all the earth, and over every creeping thing that creepeth upon the earth'" (Genesis 1:26).

If you notice, there is discussion in heaven concerning the creation of man. Look at the phrases "our image" and "our likeness." The discussion was between God the Father and God the Son. When Adam and Eve were created, they were created in the image and likeness of God. They were created in sinless perfection according to the likeness and image of God the Father and God the Son.

God created Adam first, and then he created Eve.

1. Adam—Genesis 1:27
2. Eve—Genesis 2:21–23

Before the Fall

Before the fall into sin, Adam and Eve were placed in a pristine environment called the Garden of Eden. The name Eden means "pleasure or delight." This was a place of purity since sin had not yet entered the world.

1. Eden—Genesis 2:8
2. Free to eat from all the trees—Genesis 2:16
3. The one prohibition—Genesis 2:17
4. Animals formed out of the ground as man was—Genesis 2:19
5. Adam receives Eve, which was the first marriage in the Bible—Genesis 2:21–25
6. Satan makes his first appearance—Genesis 3:1
7. Eve's big mistake: instead of rebuking Satan, she dialogued with him—Genesis 3:2–5
8. Eve submits to Satan's lies, and Adam also disobeys—Genesis 3:6–7

After the Fall

1. They both suffered shame—Genesis 3:10
2. They were now accountable for their sin—Genesis 3:11
3. The serpent would now crawl on its belly—Genesis 3:14
4. This is the first mention of a coming Savior—Genesis 3:15
5. The woman will have much pain in childbirth and be subject unto her husband—Genesis 3:16
6. The ground was cursed for Adam's sake—Genesis 3:17–18
7. Physical death was now pronounced upon the entire human race—Genesis 3:19
8. Adam and Eve lived 930 years after this pronouncement of death—Genesis 5:5

What happened to them immediately is that they died spiritually. This means that until God gives them their resurrected soul and makes them born again, they are dead to the things of God. Before you were saved, you did not concern yourself with the things of God; but after you became saved, your concern was not for things of this world. Look at the following verses:

> 1 And you *hath he quickened*, who were dead in trespasses and sins; 2 Wherein in time past ye walked according to the course of this world, according to the prince of the power of the air, the spirit that now worketh in the children of disobedience: 3 Among whom also we all had our conversation in times past in the lusts of our flesh, fulfilling the desires of the flesh and of the mind; and were by nature the children of wrath, even as others. 4 But God, who is rich in mercy, for his great love wherewith he loved us, 5 Even when we were dead in sins, hath quickened us together with Christ, (by grace ye are saved). (Ephesians 2:1–5)

The first animal sacrifice in Scripture which looked forward to the sacrifice of the Lord Jesus Christ for his people—Genesis 3:21

Adam and Eve were removed from the Garden of Eden. If they ate of the tree of life in a sinful condition, then they would be doomed to live eternally in a sinful state, which would include living with debilitating diseases and painful bodily conditions in human flesh—Genesis 3:22–24

Now every human being that is born is born in the image of Adam—Genesis 5:3

This means that when Adam was created, he was created without sin, but now every human being is born with the sin nature. Even when we become saved, we do not shed the sin nature as it lives with our new nature after the indwelling of the Holy Spirit. This creates the war within the believer between doing good and doing evil. The Apostle Paul was well aware of this situation and wrote about it in Romans 7:15–25.

Eternal results of the Fall

As a result of the fall, there are only two destinations which have been prepared for man:

1. For the unsaved: Everlasting destruction—2 Thessalonians 1:7–10
2. For the saved: Everlasting life—John 6:47

Eternal Damnation

In the previous chapter on "Man," I had mentioned that because of the fall of man into sin, there were only two eternal destinations for the human race, and that is heaven and hell. In this section, I want to look at the biblical teaching of hell or eternal damnation. The Lord Jesus Christ spoke of hell, which means it is a real place and not a place of fantasy which the unbelieving world hopes it is. Hell was originally prepared for the devil and his angels, but when Adam and Eve sinned, it became the final abode for all those in the human race without a savior.

Hell is one of the most mocked places by the world. The unbelievers talk about hell as if it is a place where many parties are going to happen, but the reality is that it is a place of eternal death where the unbeliever will reside for eternity under the wrath of God.

What Hell Is Not

There are many belief systems which have taken the seriousness of eternal damnation, and they did what they could to mollify the biblical teaching of eternal damnation.

Purgatory—This the Roman Catholic belief that when a person dies in venial sin, they go to a place for a certain number of years to have the rest of their sins purged. When they have successfully been purged of all sin, they are then allowed to enter heaven.

Now what is a venial sin? Roman Catholicism divides sin into two categories—venial and mortal. Let's say you go into a store to rob it, and in the course of the robbery, you kill the owner and three customers, which would be considered a mortal sin and means you cannot be redeemed. Let's say you go into the same store and steal a bag of potato chips, which would be considered a venial sin and can be purged after your death.

Purgatory is nowhere to be found in Scripture as it is a man-made teaching. God has redeemed those who have committed murder such as David Berkowitz who was the Son of Sam in 1976–77. I know him personally, and he is a very vibrant Christian. Then there is Tex Watson who was involved with Charles Manson in the Tate-LaBianca murders in 1969 who is also a strong Christian.

Cole Younger, who rode with the Jesse James gang in 1912, became a Christian and a preacher. Let us not forget Moses who killed the Egyptian (Exodus 2:11–12), and yet God used him to bring Israel out of Egyptian bondage. Purgatory is biblically refuted by Hebrews 8:12, 10:17–18.

Annihilation—Annihilation is taught heavily by groups such as the Jehovah's Witnesses who teach that once a person dies in an unsaved state, they are instantly annihilated and just cease to exist. This teaching is held onto by those who have unsaved relatives that have died, and if they are annihilated, then they will not suffer any of the fires of hell. A noble desire but a false one. Annihilation is biblically refuted by Matthew 18:8; Revelation 14:11; Revelation 20:11–15.

What Hell Is

A place of torment—Revelation 20:10
A place of separation—Matthew 25:41
A place of remembrance—Luke 16:25
A place for Satan and his angels—Matthew 25:41
A place of hatred—Matthew 13:50
A sealed place where no one gets out or plea bargains—Revelation 14:10–11
A place of God's wrath—Colossians 3:6
A place of darkness—Matthew 25:30

Heaven

Whenever we think of heaven, we think of the place where God lives. It is a place which is invisible to us now, but someday, we will be living there eternally. The Bible speaks of several heavens, and it is good to know the difference between them. The Lord Jesus Christ spoke more about heaven than many other subjects while he was here in his earthly ministry.

Physical Heavens

The scriptures speak about three heavens. The first two are physical, which we can see with our very eyes.

The first heaven—The first heaven is earth's atmosphere where we will see birds and airplanes fly. In the Bible, it is called the firmament, and we find its description in Genesis 1:14–18 where God created the sun to rule the day and the moon to give reflected light at night. The word *firmament* actually means expanse, which is the visible arch in the sky.

The second heaven—The second heaven would be the universe where we would see the stars and the planets. We would also see things like the Horsehead nebula or the Crab nebula. We do not know if there is an end to the universe, and if there was, what would be on the other side? The Bible records this second heaven in Job 22:12; Psalm 8:3; Matthew 24:29.

HEAVEN

God's Heaven—The Third Heaven

The third heaven is the place where God lives, and that is where the Lord Jesus Christ came from before he came to earth. It is not a physical place like the physical heavens but is a spiritual place which can never see any type of deterioration as we see in the physical heavens. The Bible calls this place the "heaven of heavens" in Deuteronomy 10:14.

Three times in scripture, it is referred to as paradise—Luke 23:43; 2 Corinthians 12:4; Revelation 2:7

There is no night in heaven—Revelation 22:5

Nothing sinful will ever enter into heaven—Revelation 21:27, 22:14–15

A place of eternal rest for the believers—Revelation 14:13

It is the promised place for the believer to live eternally—John 14:2–3

We will know each other in heaven—Matthew 17:4.

In Matthew 17:4, we see the Lord Jesus Christ and the disciples on the Mount of Transfiguration. Peter, in his impulsiveness, asked if he could make a tabernacle for Jesus, Moses, and Elijah. Moses lived 1,500 years before Peter, Elijah lived about 850 years before Peter, and yet Peter recognized both of them. This means that we will know people in heaven, even those we never met on earth.

Heaven is a place of holiness—Psalm 11:4; Habakkuk 2:20

No sorrow, death, or crying in heaven—Revelation 21:4

There is joy in heaven when a person becomes saved—Luke 15:7

Jesus ascended into the third heaven—Acts 1:11, 7:55

Heaven is only for the saved in Christ—Revelation 21:24

Sin

The word *sin* is found 336 times in the Old Testament in 299 verses. It is found 112 times in the New Testament in ninety verses. In the Old Testament, the Hebrew word for sin is *chattath*, which carries with it the meaning of "an offence or habitual sinner, one who violates the commands of the Lord."

In the New Testament, it is the Greek word *hamartia*, which carries with it the meaning of "sin, sinfulness, or a sinful deed." Sin is a prevalent theme throughout the Bible, because as we read, in the section on man, the fall in the Garden of Eden plunged the entire human race into sin. Sin is a part of every person's life. Sin is what sent the Lord Jesus Christ to the cross as a sacrifice so he could redeem those he came to save.

> And she shall bring forth a son, and thou shalt call his name JESUS: for he shall save his people from their sins. (Matthew 1:21)

The first mention of the word *sin* is found in Genesis 4:7, and the last mention of it is 1 John 5:17.

The plural word *sins* is found eighty-six times in eighty-five verses in the Old Testament and is found eighty-six times in eighty-one verses in the New Testament. Since we have the sin nature in us, it follows that we will commit sins, and as a result, we are called sinners before salvation. We must always keep in mind that we do not sin and become sinners; we commit sin because we are already sinners. Even after we are saved, we receive our new resurrected souls, but our flesh remains the same. God has redeemed us in our soul existence, but after our physical death, our flesh will go into the ground, and the real us goes into the presence of the Lord.

A good definition of sin is found in 1 John 3:4 where it states:

> Whosoever committeth sin transgresseth also the law: for sin is the transgression of the law. (1 John 3:4)

Let us just narrow an example of the above verse. Let us look at the Ten Commandments.

> Thou shalt not steal. (Exodus 20:15)

How many of us have taken things which do not belong to us? Took a pen from work? Stealing! Took a paper clip from work? Stealing! Whatever we took which is not ours is stealing. Here is another one.

> Thou shalt not commit adultery. (Exodus 20:14)

Oh, but you say, "I have never done anything like that with anyone." Well, what about in your mind?

> But I say unto you that whosoever looketh on a woman to lust after her hath committed adultery with her already in his heart. (Matthew 5:28)

The Lord Jesus widened the meaning of the commandment by stating that adultery does not have to be physical to be adultery but can be achieved in the mind without physical action. That also applies to a woman who looks on a man and lusts after him.

During the Reformation in the 1500s, a teaching had surfaced called "Total Depravity." Now this does not mean that people cannot commit acts of kindness or have compassion on other people or even do sacrificial things for people. It simply means that whatever we do is tainted by sin, which includes our actions, thoughts, desires, and even our outlook on life. Sin is so embedded in the life of every human on earth that it is literally part of our entire lives from birth to death. Here is what the Bible states about a newborn baby:

> 3 The wicked are estranged from the womb: they go astray as soon as they be born, speaking lies. 4 Their poison *is* like the poison of a serpent: *they are* like the deaf adder *that* stoppeth her ear; 5 Which will not hearken to the voice of charmers, charming never so wisely. (Psalm 58:3–5)

Not a very pretty picture of the cute little baby asleep in the crib, but it gives us insight into the very sinful nature of people and how deeply sin is imbedded in our lives right from the very beginning. Do you have to teach a five-year-old how to lie? Or does it seem to come naturally? Keep in mind the following were once babies: Hitler, Stalin, Mao Tse Tung, John Dillinger, Al Capone, Richard Speck, etc. They all grew up committing horrific crimes against society, and that is why God gives such a bleak picture of little babies, because they eventually grow up to become dreadful sinners unless they become saved.

We are going to look at some of the phases of sin from the Bible and see how heinous sin is to a thrice Holy God.

The Origin of Sin

There was only one way that sin entered into the human race. When Satan tempted Eve in the Garden of Eden, she made one major mistake, and that is instead of rebuking him for trying to get her to disobey God, she instead held a conversation with him.

We find this scenario in Genesis 3:1–7. Now we do not know how long Adam and Eve were alive before they committed their sin. They may have been alive for quite a long time from the point where God told them not to eat of the Tree of Knowledge. If this was only a short time from the time God warned them, then Eve would not have added to the words of God with the words "neither shall ye touch it," which is found in verse 3.

Satan waited until the time was right for his deception. If Adam and Eve became complacent in the Garden, then that would have been the right time for Satan to make his move. Once he did, Adam and Eve fell into sin and plunged the rest of the human race into sin.

The Extent of Sin in the World

Ever since Adam and Eve had sinned, sin had spread to the entire world. With the sin nature now in every human being, no matter where a person is born or lives, the sin nature is present.

> 2 The LORD looked down from heaven upon the children of men, to see if there were any that did understand, *and* seek God. 3 They are all gone aside, they are *all* together become filthy: *there is* none that doeth good, no, not one. (Psalm 14:2–3)

> 10 As it is written, There is none righteous, no, not one: 11 There is none that understandeth, there is none that seeketh after God. 12 They are all gone out of the way, they are together become unprofitable; there is none that doeth good, no, not one. 13 Their throat *is* an open sepulchre; with their tongues they have used deceit; the poison of asps *is* under their lips: 14 Whose mouth *is* full of cursing and bitterness: 15 Their feet *are* swift to shed blood: 16 Destruction and misery *are* in their ways: 17 And the way of peace have they not known: 18 There is no fear of God before their eyes. (Romans 3:10–18)

Notice how the Bible emphasizes the fact of the worldwide extent of sin. God tells us in both the Old and New Testaments that there is not one good person on earth. Psalms and Romans were written about a thousand years apart, which means nothing has changed. There are over seven billion people alive on this earth at present, which means there are over seven billion sin natures roaming planet earth. This includes both the reader and writer of this book, but there is one difference—salvation in Jesus Christ can control that sin nature and bring it under subjection to the new nature.

> Whereby are given unto us exceeding great and precious promises: that by these ye might be partakers of the divine nature, having escaped the corruption that is in the world through lust. (2 Peter 1:4)

Whenever we talk about sin, we must include the fruits of sin which have been numerous among man's history. We can see the manifestation of man's sinful nature just by some of his inventions, which has caused many others pain and death such as the whip, the rack, burning people alive, dunking them in boiling oil, burying them alive, thumb screws, flaying, etc. Only a person who has ignited their sinful nature would come up with tortures such as these and many others.

Is Religion Sin?

The unsaved man is in rebellion against God, and there is also a gentle side of rebellion which is just as heinous in the eyes of God, and that is religious rebellion. Now it sounds strange that religion is rebellion against God, but religion is just as evil as those who subjugate others by means of torture.

> Jesus saith unto him, "I am the way, the truth, and the life: no man cometh unto the Father, but by me." (John 14:6)

Jesus stated that he is the only way of salvation and to the Father. You became saved through the Lord Jesus Christ and no other way. Let us look at some religions and how they subtly rebel against God:

Jehovah's Witnesses—Reject Christ as the Savior.
Mormons—They claim Jesus and Satan were brothers.
Roman Catholicism—Intervention of Saints and elevation of Mary to deity.
Judaism—Rejects the Lord Jesus Christ as Messiah.
Hinduism—No good or bad, over 300 million gods.
Buddhism—Rejects Christ and calls him a mere man who was less than Buddha.
Islam—Rejects Christ as God in the flesh and teaches he is only a prophet.
New Age—Rejects physical resurrection of Christ while teaching he rose to a higher spiritual plane.
Christian Science—Jesus is the human man, and Christ is the divine idea.

As you can see, these few religions have taken the truth of God and have completely rewritten them according to their own desires. All religions are of satanic origin because they tend to lead people astray from the truth about Christ and the only way of salvation. I have just listed nine false religions, but there are countless numbers of them which are all designed to lead people astray from the truth. So you can easily see how religion can be rebellious to God because it contradicts his truth and replaces it with evil religion. Religion is more dangerous than an atomic bomb, because the atomic bomb has only a blast radius of a few miles while false religion has a radius of the entire earth.

Penalties of Sin

If there is one unifying aspect of sin, it is the penalties for sin. It does not matter whether you commit a large sin or a small sin. In God's eyes, sin is sin, and all you need is one sin to send you to an eternal hell. Now there are penalties in this life for sins which we commit as we shall see in the following biblical characters:

Adam and Eve—Banished from the Garden of Eden—Genesis 3:22–23
Miriam (sister of Moses)—became leprous for speaking against Moses—Numbers 12
Korah—Rebelled against Moses and was killed—Numbers 16:24–32
Moses—Sinned against the Lord and was not allowed to enter the Promised Land—Numbers 20:10–12; Deuteronomy 32:51–52
Nadab and Abihu—Offered strange fire before the Lord and were slain—Leviticus 10:1–2
Absalom—Rebelled against his father, King David, and was killed—2 Samuel 18:14

These eight characters from the Bible show us that there are also temporal penalties for sins committed on this earth. In addition to the earthly penalties, an unsaved person will have to answer for these sins again at the Judgment Seat of Christ on the last day. Now we have seen biblical characters who faced temporal penalties or judgments for their sin, but do we have those today? The answer is yes, and here are just a few examples:

Excessive alcohol drinking—Cirrhosis of the liver.
Sexually active outside marriage—Sexually transmitted diseases, including AIDS.
Using drugs—Addiction and even death on overdose.
Driving drunk—Loss of license and maybe loss of life.
Theft—Jail time.

These few examples will convey the idea that no one gets away with anything, even a Christian; if they commit a sin which is also against the laws of the state or country, they will face the same penalties as unbelievers. Never think you are getting away with anything, because the following Scripture teaches otherwise:

> Woe unto them that seek deep to hide their counsel from the Lord, and their works are in the dark, and they say, "Who seeth us? And who knoweth us?" (Isaiah 29:15)

Are All Sins the Same?

We tend to break sins down into categories. The Roman Catholic Church has taken sin and put them into two categories—venial and mortal. Mortal sins are not redeemable, and therefore, those who commit them are sent to eternal hell. Venial sins are smaller sins from which a person can be redeemed. These categories are not biblical and therefore are error. Even the slightest sin will cause a person to be sentenced to hell, and the reason for that is found in James 2:10.

> For whosoever shall keep the whole law, and yet offend in one point, he is guilty of all. (James 2:10)

If a person commits one sin, they are guilty of the whole law, and without a Savior, a person can expect eternal damnation. There is a great deception that people use, and they call it "white lies." The problem is that it is a lie, and liars will be judged accordingly as with any other sin. This is why salvation is so important and why we have to get the Gospel out to the world.

Final Penalty of Sin

We have already touched on this subject in the section on eternal damnation. The final penalty for sin is eternal damnation for those who do not have salvation in Christ.

> And whosoever was not found written in the book of life was cast into the lake of fire. (Revelation 20:15)

We have previously read that there are temporal penalties for committing sins, but the final penalty is the most horrifying. Those who think they can get away with committing all kinds of sin whether in private or out in public will have a rude awakening when they stand for their sins on Judgment Day.

Salvation

What Is It?

Salvation is when a person is removed from the kingdom of Satan and placed into the kingdom of God by means of receiving the Lord Jesus Christ as personal savior.

> Who hath delivered us from the power of darkness, and hath translated us into the kingdom of his dear Son: (Colossians 1:13)

When the Lord Jesus Christ went to the cross, he became the substitute atonement for the people he came to save.

> And she shall bring forth a son, and thou shalt call his name JESUS: for he shall save his people from their sins. (Matthew 1:21)

When a person became saved they are saved from the final penalty for sins. They no longer are under condemnation for sins but have eternal life.

> Verily, verily, I say unto you, he that heareth my word, and believeth on him that sent me, hath everlasting life, and shall not come into condemnation; but is passed from death unto life. (John 5:24)

They shall never be judged for their sins.

Where Did My Sins Go Upon Salvation?

Here are some of the great promises from the Scriptures concerning the fate of our sins because of Calvary.

> For I will be merciful to their unrighteousness, and their sins and their iniquities will I remember no more. (Hebrews 8:12)

> And their sins and iniquities will I remember no more. (Hebrews 10:17)

> I, even I, am he that blotteth out thy transgressions for mine own sake, and will not remember thy sins. (Isaiah 43:25)

> And they shall teach no more every man his neighbour, and every man his brother, saying, Know the LORD: for they shall all know me, from the least of them unto the greatest of them, saith the LORD: for I will forgive their iniquity, and I will remember their sin no more. (Jeremiah 31:34)

> And you, being dead in your sins and the uncircumcision of your flesh, hath he quickened together with him, having forgiven you all trespasses; {14} Blotting out the handwriting of ordinances that was against us, which was contrary to us, and took it out of the way, nailing it to his cross; (Colossians 2:13–14)

> As far as the east is from the west, so far hath he removed our transgressions from us. (Psalm 103:12)

As you can see in these seven verses, the great promises that God gives us concerns the fate of our sins upon salvation in Christ. He will blot out our sins, he will never remember our sins and iniquities, our sins were nailed to the cross of Christ, and he not only blotted them out, but he removed them from us. In other words, because of these promises of God, we will never have to worry that our sins will keep us out of heaven. Since he removed our sins, there is nothing for him to judge us for, because all our sins were paid for by the Lord Jesus Christ. This is why God can say the following found in Isaiah 55:1:

> Ho, every one that thirsteth, come ye to the waters, and he that hath no money; come ye, buy, and eat; yea, come, buy wine and milk without money and without price. (Isaiah 55:1)

The reason they can buy without money is because the price was already paid by Christ.

Why Is Salvation Necessary?

Salvation is necessary because no one can get to heaven without becoming saved in Christ. The Lord Jesus Christ is the only way to heaven, and although there are hundreds of religions out there, none can get you to heaven.

> Jesus saith unto him, "I am the way, the truth, and the life: no man cometh unto the Father, but by me." (John 14:6)

Many religions believe they can bypass Jesus and go directly to the Father, but that cannot and will never happen.

Is Salvation a Process?

There are many world religions that claim you must go through certain rituals or you must adhere to their set of rules and regulations to get to heaven. Salvation is not a process, because a person becomes saved instantly. When a person receives the Lord Jesus Christ as their personal savior, they are saved at that moment for eternity. There is no process or procedures to follow since salvation is in God's hands and not ours.

> But I will sacrifice unto thee with the voice of thanksgiving; I will pay that that I have vowed. Salvation is of the LORD. (Jonah 2:9)

Back in the Old Testament in the book of Jonah, the prophet Jonah writes that salvation is of the Lord. It is verses like this which show how the Bible is one cohesive whole.

Does Salvation Require Any Good Works?

If salvation required a person to do any good works, then salvation would be by works and not by grace.

> 8 For by grace are ye saved through faith; and that not of yourselves: it is the gift of God: 9 Not of works, lest any man should boast. (Ephesians 2:8–9)

The next question would be how many good works and what types of good works? No one can work for salvation, because Christ paid the entire penalty for our sins. If a person believes they have to do good works for salvation, then they are basically stating that the sacrifice of Christ was not sufficient enough for our salvation and that man has to add to it. That would be tantamount to blasphemy, because it was God, the Son, who removed our sins from us, and to say that we could do a better job than he did is total wickedness. Now do good works play a part in the life of a Christian?

> For we are his workmanship, created in Christ Jesus unto good works, which God hath before

ordained that we should walk in them. (Ephesians 2:10)

Once we become saved, then we partake in doing good works which could be giving to ministries or passing out tracts or some other type of ministry. This is why I included a chapter on spiritual gifts, because it is these that the Lord gave to empower us and to engage in the right ministry which the Lord will guide us into according to the way he has gifted us.

Must One Repent as a Requirement for Salvation?

Repentance means a "change of mind" toward something. When we repent of sins, it means we have changed our minds about it. At one time, we thought a particular sin was fine, but when we became saved, we now realize that the sin was against the teachings of Scripture and we decide to never partake in that sin again. Now repentance for salvation would also constitute a work, which means before I can become saved, I must repent of my sins. This is also an error, because a person before salvation is still dead in their sins, and therefore, a dead person cannot do anything but be dead.

> And you, being dead in your sins and the uncircumcision of your flesh, hath he quickened together with him, having forgiven you all trespasses; (Colossians 2:13)

As we read in Colossians 2:13, a person before salvation is dead in their sins. Biblical repentance is also a gift from God and is another way of saying salvation.

> In meekness instructing those that oppose themselves; if God peradventure will give them repentance to the acknowledging of the truth; (2 Timothy 2:25)

In 2 Timothy 2:25, we read that it is God who gives repentance, just as it is God who gives salvation. After a person becomes saved, then they are able to repent of their sins, because they will have the ability to see that sinning in any form is wrong.

How Does a Person Become Saved?

We have seen that a person cannot do any kind of good works to obtain salvation nor does repenting of their sins lead to salvation. The way a person becomes saved is through the grace of God. Now I mentioned grace in a previous section, so what is it? The technical meaning of grace is "the unmerited favor of God." In other words, you were chosen by God, not because you did something to deserve it, but you were chosen because God has a plan for your life both here and in the next life.

Why God chooses one and not another is a great mystery. All those who believe today and will believe in Christ in the future were chosen from before the foundation of the world.

> According as he hath chosen us in him before the foundation of the world, that we should be holy and without blame before him in love: (Ephesians 1:4)

Therefore, since God chose us before the foundation of the world, there is no such thing as us accepting him. As you continue in your Christian walk, you will hear phrases like "accept the Lord" or "ask him into your life, etc." These are unbiblical and cannot be found anywhere in Scripture. Since God has named you for salvation before the foundation of the world, he has also named a certain time when you will become saved.

For me, I became saved when I was twenty-seven years old. For everyone, the timing may be different and the circumstances may be different. Some are saved within tragic circumstances, and some are saved without any special or tragic circumstances. Salvation is in the hands of God, not ours.

SALVATION

Since Adam and Eve sinned, the whole human race was plunged into sin, and with that sin came spiritual death. The way God saves us is that those who are named for salvation at their appointed time, God takes from the point of spiritual death and gives them their resurrected soul. The reason it is called a resurrected soul is because just like when someone is physically dead, such as Lazarus in John 11, Jesus raised him from the dead, that was called a "resurrection." In like manner, God takes our dead souls and raises them from the dead and indwells us with the Holy Spirit who gives us life eternal.

> Who also hath made us able ministers of the new testament; not of the letter, but of the spirit: for the letter killeth, but the spirit giveth life. (2 Corinthians 3:6)

Once we are saved and have the Holy Spirit dwelling in us, then we have faith to believe in Christ, because faith is a fruit of the Holy Spirit.

> But the fruit of the Spirit is love, joy, peace, longsuffering, gentleness, goodness, faith. (Galatians 5:22)

Those who are not saved cannot believe in Christ, and that is why when you speak with those who are unsaved, they will look at you strange and not understand the things you are saying, because those who are saved speak on a different level than those who are unsaved. So just to recap, you become saved and then you receive your resurrected souls and you are indwelled by the Holy Spirit and you now have the ability to believe in Christ and the things of God. This all takes place in an instant at the moment of salvation.

There is a group called charismatics who teach that a person does not receive the fullness of the Holy Spirit at salvation, but it comes at a later time. This is false and unbiblical.

> 3 Blessed be the God and Father of our Lord Jesus Christ, who hath blessed us with all spir-

itual blessings in heavenly places in Christ: (Ephesians 1:3)

As you can read in Ephesians 1:3, we have been blessed with "all" spiritual blessings; in other words, God did not withhold anything from us until a later time. He gave it all to us at the moment of salvation. We just learn to develop those blessings and use them as we go along in our Christian walk.

Can We Know We Are Saved?

There are many religions, even churches who cannot guarantee you that you can know you are saved, and some even claim you are arrogant if you claim you can know. These people who claim this walk in darkness, because the Bible is very clear that we can know if we are saved.

> These things have I written unto you that believe on the name of the Son of God; that ye may know that ye have eternal life, and that ye may believe on the name of the Son of God. (1 John 5:13)

1 John 5:13 states in no uncertain terms that we can know we are saved, and the reason God wants us to know we are saved is so we can be encouraged all the time we have on earth and not continue wondering if we are saved. The Bible is very supportive of those who are saved and continues to encourage us in our walk. So never let anyone tell you that you cannot know if you are saved, because the Bible tells us that we can know, and that strengthens the believer every single day. Another reason God wants us to know we are saved is because that knowledge propels us into continuing on in ministry without any apprehension.

SALVATION

Can We Lose Our Salvation?

One of the most evil beliefs which is courted by many Christians is the belief that one can lose their salvation. First of all, a Christian did not work for their salvation and, therefore, cannot work to lose it. Secondly, the person who died on the cross was not just a mere man but the Son of God who took upon himself the sins of all those he came to save, and we previously saw that all our sins were removed from us and that God had blotted out our sins for his sake. If all our sins are removed and blotted out, then how could we lose our salvation since sin is the only thing that can send a person to hell? The reality is the loss of salvation is nowhere found in the scriptures, because it is a man-made teaching. Once God has saved us, we are saved for eternity.

The phrase "everlasting life" is used eleven times in the Scriptures: Daniel 12:2; Matthew 19:29; John 3:16, 3:36, 4:14, 5:24, 6:27, 6:40, 6:47; Acts 13:46; Romans 6:22. Look up each of these verses and familiarize yourself with them.

The phrase "eternal life" is used twenty-six times in the Scriptures: Matthew 19:16; Mark 10:17, 10:30; Luke 10:25, 18:18; John 3:15, 5:39, 6:54, 6:68, 10:28, 17:2; Acts 13:48; Romans 2:7, 5:21, 6:23; 1 Timothy 6:12, 6:19; Titus 1:2, 3:7; 1 John 1:2, 2:25, 3:15, 5:11, 5:13, 5:20; Jude 21. Look up these verses and familiarize yourself with them.

It is important to understand that we just listed eleven verses where the term "everlasting life" is found and twenty-six verses where "eternal life" is found. This means that thirty-seven verses mention eternal and everlasting life. If a person could lose their salvation, then these thirty-seven verses would be a false teaching. If a person could lose their salvation, then these thirty-seven verses should read "temporary" life.

The great truth of Scripture concerning eternal life for the Christian is that eternal life begins at the moment of salvation and not at the moment of physical death. What happens at physical death is that the soul returns to the Lord, and our physical bodies get buried. When this happens, we will be more alive than we are right now, because we will not have a body attached to us which lusts after sin. At this point, let us look at some scripture verses which show plainly that a true Christian cannot lose their salvation.

> All that the Father giveth me shall come to me; and him that cometh to me I will in no wise cast out. {38} For I came down from heaven, not to do mine own will, but the will of him that sent me. {39} And this is the Father's will which hath sent me, that of all which he hath given me I should lose nothing, but should raise it up again at the last day. (John 6:37–39)

Here are some verses which plainly teach that the Lord Jesus will not lose one person, plus he will not cast any out. Notice that in verse 37, there is no exception clause. Jesus states that he will cast none of his true children out because he is the one who bought them with his own blood.

> Take heed therefore unto yourselves, and to all the flock, over the which the Holy Ghost hath made you overseers, to feed the church of God, which he hath purchased with his own blood. (Acts 20:28)

He doesn't say that if you do a certain sin or a number of sins, then you get thrown out. He will not cast out nor will he lose one soul.

> The Lord is not slack concerning his promise, as some men count slackness; but is longsuffering to us-ward, not willing that any should perish, but that all should come to repentance. (2 Peter 3:9)

This verse has been misused by all in the freewill camp that it is God's will that no one should perish. It is used with the understanding that God doesn't want anyone going to hell, and that is why a person needs to accept Christ. This verse is not speaking about a general call to mankind but is speaking about the elect of God. It is God's will that none of those he has chosen before the foundation of the world will perish. If God names a person to salvation during their lifetime, God will intervene and save them. This is God's will—that none of his chosen will ever perish. This is why those who are truly saved will never be cast out or lost, because God's will for their lives is eternal salvation.

> And I give unto them eternal life; and they shall never perish, neither shall any man pluck them out of my hand. (John 10:28)

This verse tells us that we have eternal life. The term "eternal life" as we previously saw is found twenty-six times in the New Testament. If the believer has eternal life, and we shall never perish, then how can some teach that we have temporary life in Christ? It is a wrong assumption on the part of many who feel they must work for their salvation.

Eternal life begins at the moment a person becomes truly saved and not at the moment of death. What looks like a person losing their salvation is when a person makes some kind of verbal profession, and then they quickly go back into their former lifestyle, having never been truly regenerated. So those who believe that a person can lose their salvation looks at this person and thinks they have living proof of that teaching.

The truth is, if a person never becomes saved, they cannot live the regenerated life. This verse also tells us that Jesus gives eternal life that it is not something that we work for. No one shall pluck or take us out of the hand of the Lord Jesus either. Once we are given eternal life, there are no breaches in it nor any way to lose it.

> Now before the feast of the Passover, when Jesus knew that his hour was come that he should depart out of this world unto the Father, having

loved his own which were in the world, he loved them unto the end. (John 13:1)

In this verse, we are reminded that Jesus loves his own. He is not saying that he loves everyone in the world but that he loves his own and he loves them unto the end. Whenever we see God or Jesus loving someone, it is always a synonym for salvation. The love of Christ for the believer continues into the new heaven and the new earth. There is not one passage in Scripture where it teaches that God loves the unbeliever. On the contrary, he hates the workers of iniquity.

> The foolish shall not stand in thy sight: thou hatest all workers of iniquity. (Psalm 5:5 KJV)

This verse is avoided by those who teach the universal love of God for all mankind. So when we compare the two Scriptures, we see that there is love for the believer but an abhorrence of the unbeliever. If a person could lose their salvation by sinning, then Jesus would not be able to love them to the end; then he would only be able to love them till their next sin. This is not taught anywhere in Scripture.

> I have manifested thy name unto the men which thou gavest me out of the world: thine they were, and thou gavest them me; and they have kept thy word. (John 17:6)

> I pray for them: I pray not for the world, but for them which thou hast given me; for they are thine. {10} And all mine are thine, and thine are mine; and I am glorified in them. (John 17:9–10)

> Neither pray I for these alone, but for them also which shall believe on me through their word. (John 17:20)

SALVATION

These particular verses confirm what was taught in John 6:37–39. God the Father draws people to the Lord Jesus Christ, and then they become saved. We also see that Jesus is praying for those who are his and is not praying for the unbelievers. The Lord Jesus Christ is not glorified in the unbeliever, only in the believer. Jesus prays for the disciples, plus he also includes those that will be saved through their word which points to future generations.

> For I am persuaded, that neither death, nor life, nor angels, nor principalities, nor powers, nor things present, nor things to come, {39} Nor height, nor depth, nor any other creature, shall be able to separate us from the love of God, which is in Christ Jesus our Lord. (Romans 8:38–39)

These are some of the most powerful verses in Scripture which teach that a believer can never be separated from God. This means that no matter what happens to the believer, they can never be separated nor lose their salvation. The love of God is a synonym for salvation as we have previously seen.

> For the gifts and calling of God are without repentance. (Romans 11:29)

The term "without repentance" means "irrevocable." When God saves someone, that calling and gift of salvation to that believer is not revocable. That is because God is only saving those whom he named before the foundation of the world. This is why salvation cannot be revoked. As stated previously, salvation is applied only to those whom God has chosen and salvation is not an "offer" to the world. The following three verses teach this truth very plainly.

> And all that dwell upon the earth shall worship him, whose names are not written in the book of life of the Lamb slain from the foundation of the world. (Revelation 13:8)

> The beast that thou sawest was, and is not; and shall ascend out of the bottomless pit, and go into perdition: and they that dwell on the earth shall wonder, whose names were not written in the book of life from the foundation of the world, when they behold the beast that was, and is not, and yet is. (Revelation 17:8)

> For we which have believed do enter into rest, as he said, As I have sworn in my wrath, if they shall enter into my rest: although the works were finished from the foundation of the world. (Hebrews 4:3)

Here are two verses from Isaiah which plainly teach that whatever God sets out to do, he will accomplish it, and no one can thwart his plans.

> For the LORD of hosts hath purposed, and who shall disannul it? and his hand is stretched out, and who shall turn it back? (Isaiah 14:27)

> Yea, before the day was I am he; and there is none that can deliver out of my hand: I will work, and who shall let it? (Isaiah 43:13)

When he speaks of being delivered out of his hands, it means that nothing can be taken from him. We saw this principle taught in John 6:37–39 that the Lord Jesus will lose no one. In Isaiah 43:13, "who shall let it" may be understood as "who can turn it back."

If God saves a person, then who, including that person that God saved, has the power to reverse God's work? I don't know anyone powerful enough to do that. Do you? Certainly sin cannot hold more power than God.

> Moreover the law entered, that the offence might abound. But where sin abounded, grace did much more abound: (Romans 5:20)

So here we see that not even sin has the power to fracture grace. Knowing this, how can a person believe that they can lose their salvation if they sin? They can believe it only through biblical ignorance or willful evasion of the truth.

> For by grace are ye saved through faith; and that not of yourselves: it is the gift of God: {9} Not of works, lest any man should boast. (Ephesians 2:8–9)

Here are probably two of the most used, yet misunderstood, verses. Those who teach that you must accept Christ as Savior misuse the verse, although maybe not intentionally. There are many pastors and theologians who know that salvation is by grace alone yet attach a work to it. That work being a person having to take an action by "accepting Christ." Even though it does not look like a work, in God's sight, it is adding to the salvation plan. Any addition of even a minute's work makes it an adulterated grace.

As we have previously seen, God applies the grace of salvation to those he has predestined, and there is no work on the part of the individual receiving salvation. This means that if a person received salvation without the addition of any work, then there is no work that anyone can do to lose it. Sin is a work of evil, but nevertheless, it is a work. Therefore, since it is impossible to work for salvation, it is also impossible to lose salvation by any sinful work.

> And grieve not the holy Spirit of God, whereby ye are sealed unto the day of redemption. (Ephesians 4:30)

This verse teaches us that the believer is sealed unto the day of redemption, which will either be the return of the Lord or the believer's home going. The term *grieve* carries with it the meaning of "sorrow." We are being admonished to refrain from sin because sin grieves the Holy Spirit. If you notice, the Holy Spirit is grieved when we sin, but the Scripture does not say that he will leave us if we sin.

This is because we are eternally sealed by the Holy Spirit. If the Holy Spirit stays with us during a time of sin and does not leave us, that means we cannot lose our salvation since he is still dwelling in us. Only those without the Holy Spirit are unsaved.

> But ye are not in the flesh, but in the Spirit, if so be that the Spirit of God dwell in you. Now if any man have not the Spirit of Christ, he is none of his. (Romans 8:9 KJV)

> For ye are dead, and your life is hid with Christ in God. (Colossians 3:3)

This verse teaches us that the believer has died and their life is now hidden in Christ. The believer's identity is with the Lord Jesus Christ. The words "is hid" is the Greek word *krupto*, which carries with it the meaning of "kept secret and kept safe." So this verse is telling us that we are kept safe and secret in the Lord Jesus Christ. Remember the passages of John 6:37–39 where Jesus stated that he will lose none? Now we know why, because our eternal lives are kept safe and secret with the Lord Jesus Christ. How is it possible for sin to be able to break that safekeeping by eternal God himself? It is impossible.

> For I will be merciful to their unrighteousness, and their sins and their iniquities will I remember no more. (Hebrews 8:12)

> And their sins and iniquities will I remember no more. (Hebrews 10:17)

> I, even I, am he that blotteth out thy transgressions for mine own sake, and will not remember thy sins. (Isaiah 43:25)

> And they shall teach no more every man his neighbour, and every man his brother, saying, Know the LORD: for they shall all know me, from the least of them unto the greatest of them, saith the LORD: for I will forgive their iniquity, and I will remember their sin no more. (Jeremiah 31:34)

I wish to repost four verses from a previous section which carry the theme of the impossibility of loss of salvation. These four verses all carry with them the same theme. When God forgives a person of their sins, he has elected to forget those sins. Nowhere in Scripture is it written that God chooses to remember our sins, thus causing a loss of salvation. When God removes our sins, he annihilates them. In other words, they can never be held against us.

> And you, being dead in your sins and the uncircumcision of your flesh, hath he quickened together with him, having forgiven you all trespasses; {14} Blotting out the handwriting of ordinances that was against us, which was contrary to us, and took it out of the way, nailing it to his cross; (Colossians 2:13–14)

Notice in these verses, we read that *all* trespasses have been forgiven. God's perfect and holy law was satisfied (handwriting of ordinances), which means there will be no more penalty for sins committed by a believer. Some will object by asking, "What about sins committed in the future?"

When Colossians 2:13–14 was written, which was about 60–64 AD, where were you? You were not scheduled to be born for another nineteen centuries. This would mean that all the sins you were forgiven for were not even committed yet. Those sins that you are yet to commit in the future have all been blotted out by Christ. When God applied grace to you, it carried the full effect of the atonement of Christ, which means every sin you have committed or will commit has been blotted out. You don't have a sin to your name before God.

> And in their mouth was found no guile: for they are without fault before the throne of God. (Revelation 14:5)

If you still cling to the belief that you can lose your salvation, then you are also under the belief that the atonement of Christ was insufficient, thereby forcing you to save yourself. The idea of insufficient atonement is a blasphemy against Christ and God's salvation plan. To say that the sinless Christ can't save you, but your sinful works can, is the height of evil arrogance.

> But this man, after he had offered one sacrifice for sins forever, sat down on the right hand of God; {13} From henceforth expecting till his enemies be made his footstool. {14} For by one offering he hath perfected forever them that are sanctified. (Hebrews 10:12–14)

In these verses, we read that the atonement of Christ perfected those who are sanctified. The term *sanctified* is another synonym for *salvation*. In Scripture, we only read of God sanctifying the believer. The Greek word which underlies *sanctified* is the same word for *holy*. Never does God refer to an unbeliever as holy. The word *perfected* means to "make perfect, complete." This is what the Lord Jesus Christ did for the believer. We are now complete in Christ. The one sacrifice has perfected the believer forever. That eternal sanctification and completeness begins at the moment a person becomes saved and continues right into eternity. If a person could lose their salvation, that would mean they would lose their holiness, but this verse teaches that the perfecting is forever and not a temporary intermittent time period.

> To an inheritance incorruptible, and undefiled, and that fadeth not away, reserved in heaven for you. (1 Peter 1:4)

In this verse, we read that a place is reserved for the believer in heaven. The word *reserved* carries with it the meaning of *preserved*. Now if a believer could lose their salvation, why would God promise his children that there is a place reserved for them in heaven? If salvation was in the hands of man, then God would be in heaven waiting to see if a person makes it. He would not be able to promise that a place is reserved for anyone if they can lose their salvation for any reason. This verse is an assurance that since the Lord Jesus Christ atoned for the sins of his people, they are assured a place in heaven.

> Who are kept by the power of God through faith unto salvation ready to be revealed in the last time. (1 Peter 1:5)

This verse teaches us that the believer is not on their own, exercising their spiritual abilities. We learn that God "keeps" his children through his power. The word *kept* carries with it the meaning of "guarded" and is in the present tense. So here we have God guarding his children through his power. What power on earth is capable of superseding the power of God? I know of none. Sin can never be stronger than the power of God!

How Does God View the Believer?

Now that we have become saved, the Christian has a much different relationship with God. Before we were saved, we were enemies of God because we were in the kingdom of Satan. Now that we have been transferred out of the kingdom of Satan, we have become a child of God and no longer are we at war with God but instead are children of God.

> Therefore being justified by faith, we have peace with God through our Lord Jesus Christ. (Romans 5:1)

The war is now over, and we are at peace with God through Christ.

Many times, you will hear Christians say that "we are just sinners saved by grace" with a hint of false humility. Okay, I challenge them to find that saying in Scripture! I will give you a hint. You cannot find it! Why? It doesn't exist in Scripture. It has become one of those unbiblical sayings that sounds oh so religious and humble. It is a very misleading statement, because Christ did not die on the cross to make us sinners. He died to free us from the effects and penalty of sins. God has a special relationship with his children and makes no bones about how he views us. The Scriptures give us beautiful descriptions of how God views us. I want to show the beautiful relationship which exists between God and his children.

There are many Christians who walk under a cloud of condemnation, simply because many pastors do not understand our relationship to God "our" Father and pass that ignorance onto the sheep. My goal is to acclimate Christians to the Scriptures. Christians must rediscover the Bible without the folly of theology books telling them what we shall believe. This chapter is written to aid new Christians in their understanding about their relationship to God. I would like to look at one of the most significant chapters in Scripture dealing with "How God Views His Children." We will discuss Ephesians chapter one, and when we have completed this chapter, you may be surprised how God views you if you are a true child of God.

Many Christians are ignorant of how God views them. This is not a slanderous statement but a stark reality owing to the high rate of biblical illiteracy in the church and among individual Christians. In today's church, psychological teachings are usurping the teaching of pure Scripture. The next time you hear a sermon, listen carefully, and you will hear much psychological dogma mixed with Scripture and presented to you as absolute truth and authority.

The sad result is that many Christians do not know how wonderfully they stand with God because of their relationship to Christ. I feel sorry for those Christians who are told every Sunday that they are nothing but rotten sinners that should have gone to hell. This kind of teaching from the pulpit on a continual basis tends to tear believers down instead of build them up.

No Christian should fear God in the sense that he is a despotic ruler who waits for us to mess up so he could zap us. God is not a vengeful God toward his children. His wrath is reserved for the unbeliever on Judgment Day.

> Seeing it is a righteous thing with God to recompense tribulation to them that trouble you; {7} And to you who are troubled rest with us, when the Lord Jesus shall be revealed from heaven with his mighty angels, {8} In flaming fire taking vengeance on them that know not God, and that obey not the gospel of our Lord Jesus Christ: {9} Who shall be punished with everlasting destruction from the presence of the Lord, and from the

> glory of his power; {10} When he shall come to be glorified in his saints, and to be admired in all them that believe (because our testimony among you was believed) in that day. (2 Thessalonians 1:6–10)

I do not want to convey the mistaken notion that man is inherently good and deserves heaven, but as I have already mentioned, when we become saved, our relationship to God changes. We are no longer a sinner under Satan's authority but a Saint under God's authority.

If one reads the Scriptures carefully, especially in Genesis 3, we find that because of Adam and Eve's sin, the whole human race was sentenced to hell; yet, God in his mercy has chosen to save millions from hell. Why doesn't he save everyone? I cannot answer that, and neither can anyone else. The fact remains that if God has saved you, you have a tremendous relationship with him.

I will take some keywords and phrases out of our Scripture passages to help focus our study, but I ask that you read the entire chapter. When you come to the words we will study, you will have the definition and will gain a deeper insight of how God views his children.

Ephesians 1

"Paul, an apostle of Jesus Christ by the will of God, to the saints which are at Ephesus, and to the faithful in Christ Jesus" (Ephesians 1:1).

The word *saints* may be translated "dedicated, set apart, sacred or holy." God views each Christian as one who is sacred and holy. This brings us into a special relationship with God. I have seen too many preachers and Christians who have been saved for many years espousing the belief that we are just sinners saved by grace. We need to start viewing ourselves as God views us. Let's do a brief analysis of that saying.

The truth is that we were classified as sinners before salvation, and this is how God viewed us. Upon salvation, we received "positional holiness." If I am just a sinner saved by grace, then I would be in a confusing situation. If I am a sinner, then I am not saved by grace, and if I am saved by grace, then I am not a sinner. The sinner in scripture is one who is unsaved and living in a state of perpetual sin. Remember, we are approaching this from God's point of view as written in Scripture. "Sinner saved by grace" cannot be found anywhere in Scripture in reference to God's attitude toward his children.

Let me say here that all Christians do sin, but because of Calvary, all those sins have been erased and not held against us anymore. Christ's sacrifice paid for every sin that I ever committed or will commit in the future. If just one sin is held against me, then I am destined for hell and was never saved. This is why it is important to know the difference between being a sinner and one who has the ability to sin. The unbeliever is classified as a sinner since everything they do is sin. The Christian is called saint, and the sooner we start thinking like saints, instead of sinners, we will begin to see our Christian lives blossom.

The abundant life which Christ came to give us is not on the spiritual level of those who still view themselves as sinners but those who realize that God has elevated their position to saint. If God views us as holy, it is blasphemy against the cross of Christ to continue to view ourselves as sinners. If you believe that line of thought, you are also believing that Christ's death on that cross was not sufficient to take away your sin. In essence, that would mean sin and Satan are stronger than God. With thought patterns like these, no wonder many Christians have stopped growing.

Always keep in mind it is what God says that sets truth, not what we feel or believe. Ponder this for a minute: if I am still a sinner, then I should consider myself a "holy sinner." These two words are oil and water, and no amount of homogenization will ever mix them. If you are saved, God no longer views you as a sinner; so why should you continue believing a statement right out of the pits of the camp of false humility?

> Paul, an apostle of Jesus Christ by the will of God, to the saints which are at Ephesus, and to the faithful in Christ Jesus. (Ephesians 1:1)

The word *faithful* may also be translated "a believer, a faithful one, trustworthy, or one on whom we may rely." Here, God views his children as reliable. The Greek word *pistos* is also translated *believer* in 1 Timothy 4:2, *faithful* in Hebrews 2:17, and *true* in 1 Timothy 3:1. Since God has given us the Holy Spirit, he has entrusted his spiritual riches to us, which is the gospel. God views us as responsible enough to deliver the gospel worldwide.

God has also given us the faith to believe in him, because man with a sin-permeated mind could never believe in God on his own. God implants in us the desire to be faithful so his work on earth could be completed to his glory. We may not feel faithful all the time, but again, what has God written in the Bible? Don't take my word for it, use a concordance and a King James Bible and do your own study on our focus words in this chapter.

We must never trust our feelings, because many times, we may not feel saved. Just because I do not feel saved does not mean I am not. If God says I'm saved, I'm saved! Matter settled! God does not work according to our feelings. The hymn we sing at Christmas, which refers to only Christians, is, "O Come All Ye Faithful."

2 Timothy 2:2 states we shall commit the gospel to "faithful men." The word used here is *pistos*. What God seems to be telling us is that he has empowered us through the Holy Spirit to take the true gospel to the ends of the earth. So God views you—*yes, you*—as part of his reliable and responsible army of believers! Put this book down and start thanking him, but pick it back up again, because there is more to come.

> Grace be to you, and peace, from God our Father,
> and from the Lord Jesus Christ. (Ephesians 1:2)

The Greek word *eirene* is translated *peace* throughout the New Testament, except in three places. The first place is Acts 7:26 where it is rendered "one again" which carries the meaning of reunification of two which were separated. The second place is Acts 9:31 where it is rendered *rest*, which carries the idea of a state of peace, tranquility with the inducement of a state of security. The third place is Acts

HOW DOES GOD VIEW THE BELIEVER?

24:2 where it is rendered *quietness*, which also carries with it the idea of a place of security and repose. The regular translation of *eirene* into peace carries with it the idea of inner peace resulting from forgiveness and a renewed relationship with God.

> Therefore being justified by faith, we have peace with God through our Lord Jesus Christ, (Romans 5:1)

We see in this one word how God views the believer as being reunited with him. Sin separated the whole human race from God, but the cross of Christ has given reconciliation to every believer. The word also reveals we have a state of security. God views the believer as being secure in him, no matter what the outward circumstances are.

> For ye are dead, and your life is hid with Christ in God. (Colossians 3:3)

God gives his children quietness and sweet repose. Remember the pastoral promise in Psalm 23:2? "He maketh me to lie down in green pastures: he leadeth me beside the still waters." God gives inward peace in an age of chaos.

> Blessed be the God and Father of our Lord Jesus Christ, who hath blessed us with all spiritual blessings in heavenly places in Christ. (Ephesians 1:3)

Every spiritual need the believer has on earth was already supplied. The word *blessing* is the Greek word *eulogia* which means "good speaking, praise." God has given his praises to those in Christ Jesus. We literally have a divine commendation as we read in Romans 2:29, "But he is a Jew, which is one inwardly; and circumcision is that of the heart, in the spirit, and not in the letter; whose praise is not of men, but of God."

This verse speaks of the believer as being praised by God because of our relationship to his Son. This is not to imply that God worships man, because that would be outright blasphemy. God was well-pleased with Christ, and because of Christ, he is well-pleased with the Christian. Nowhere in the Bible do we find that God is pleased with the sinner.

Remember, we are beginning to see how God views the believer, and we must do this from a biblical perspective. Program your mind to think biblically, and you will begin to think as God thinks to the extent that a human is able to do so.

> According as he hath chosen us in him before the foundation of the world, that we should be holy and without blame before him in love. (Ephesians 1:4)

The word *chosen* comes from the Greek word *eklegomai* which means to "select, choose, elect." Here we read that God has literally handpicked every Christian.

> All that the Father giveth me shall come to me; and him that cometh to me I will in no wise cast out. (John 6:37)

Man did not choose God but God chose man.

> But as many as received him, to them gave he power to become the sons of God, even to them that believe on his name: {13} Which were born, not of blood, nor of the will of the flesh, nor of the will of man, but of God. (John 1:12–13)

This may be borne out with many other Scriptures. For a Christian to proclaim "I have accepted the Lord" is a misnomer, since it is God who accepted us, the reprobate sinner. When we begin to realize that it was God who saved us and it was not by our own action, we will have a better appreciation of our salvation since we realize we had no part in it.

When we know that God reached down and chose the Christian, we will have more desire to serve him in whatever capacity he chooses. The normal teaching is that God waits for the sinner to accept or reject Christ. This will never occur since man is spiritually dead (Eph. 2:1–3). If a person is dead, how is it possible to hear, never mind respond? We respond because God opens our spiritual ears, making us aware we are sinners and that we need a savior; it is none of man's doing. God has chosen you to be his child. What will you do with the life he has given you?

> According as he hath chosen us in him before
> the foundation of the world, that we should
> be holy and without blame before him in love.
> (Ephesians 1:4)

The same root word in the Greek is used for both "saint" and "holy." If God says we are holy, how can we just be sinners?

> According as he hath chosen us in him before
> the foundation of the world, that we should
> be holy and without blame before him in love:
> (Ephesians 1:4)

The words "without blame" may be translated "without blemish of sin, disgrace, or blameless." This phrase shows how unscriptural the phrase "sinner saved by grace" is when describing the Christian, because God is stating he views us as having no blemish of sin. Because of Christ, God sees us as pure, without sin, even though that is not how we see ourselves. Remember, it is not our preprogrammed thoughts that count, but it is the Bible which is the final authority. Two good commentaries on this verse are found in Romans 8:33 and Revelation 14:4–5:

> Who shall lay anything to the charge of God's
> elect? It is God that justifieth. (Romans 8:33)

> These are they which were not defiled with women; for they are virgins. These are they which follow the Lamb whithersoever he goeth. These were redeemed from among men, being the first fruits unto God and to the Lamb. {5} And in their mouth was found no guile: for they are without fault before the throne of God. (Revelation 14:4–5)

God is the one who declares the Christian to be free of sin, and we better start analyzing the pet sayings we hear. God has declared his children sinless because of Christ. Let me emphasize because we sin after salvation, God does not view us as sinners. I challenge anyone to show me in the Bible where God calls redeemed saints "sinners saved by grace." If we were not declared sinless, we would be on our way to hell, not heaven, because it takes only one sin to send us there.

> Having predestinated us unto the adoption of children by Jesus Christ to himself, according to the good pleasure of his will, (Ephesians 1:5)

The word *predestinated* may also be translated "predetermined, foreordain, or decree beforehand." This one word reveals to us that we were already in God's plan eons ago. God chose to save you and he predetermined your life as he did for Jeremiah, Paul, and John the Baptist:

> Before I formed thee in the belly I knew thee; and before thou camest forth out of the womb I sanctified thee, and I ordained thee a prophet unto the nations. (Jeremiah 1:5)

> But when it pleased God, who separated me from my mother's womb, and called me by his grace, (Galatians 1:15)

> But the angel said unto him, Fear not, Zacharias: for thy prayer is heard; and thy wife Elisabeth shall bear thee a son, and thou shalt call his name John. {14} And thou shalt have joy and gladness; and many shall rejoice at his birth. {15} For he shall be great in the sight of the Lord, and shall drink neither wine nor strong drink; and he shall be filled with the Holy Ghost, even from his mother's womb. {16} And many of the children of Israel shall he turn to the Lord their God. {17} And he shall go before him in the spirit and power of Elias, to turn the hearts of the fathers to the children, and the disobedient to the wisdom of the just; to make ready a people prepared for the Lord. (Luke 1:13–17)

This is where election comes in. Because of Adam's sin, the whole human race was condemned to hell, yet God in his mercy predestined millions to be saved. Why he doesn't save everyone is unknown to us, but God's holiness must be vindicated since it was man's freewill in Eden which caused all that sin and suffering throughout the ages.

Thank God he saves us without our consent or else none would become saved, because we love our sins more than anything.

> And this is the condemnation, that light is come into the world, and men loved darkness rather than light, because their deeds were evil. (John 3:19)

> As it is written, There is none righteous, no, not one: {11} There is none that understandeth, there is none that seeketh after God. (Romans 3:10–11)

If you are a Christian, then God has predestinated you for heaven, so let us not argue doctrine and just thank him. We have just seen that predestination is a doctrine of Scripture, not an invention of John Calvin.

> Having predestinated us unto the adoption of children by Jesus Christ to himself, according to the good pleasure of his will, (Ephesians 1:5)

When God saves us, he transfers us from the family of Satan to the family of God and gives us full rights as if we were natural children. He makes us an heir of all things and gives us his family name, Christian.

> And if children, then heirs; heirs of God, and joint-heirs with Christ; if so be that we suffer with him, that we may be also glorified together. (Romans 8:17)

The name "Christian" carries with it the meaning of "being attached to or an adherent of Christ."

God shows us we are his children and are in his family with permission to call him Father. This means he expects us to pray and speak with him, to love and understand him. Since we are his children, we should read his word with joy, because it is like receiving a letter from home. Many believers do not understand their relationship between God and themselves. When Christians study the Bible more intently, they will see God's intentions toward them are not hostile but loving.

> For I know the thoughts that I think toward you, saith the LORD, thoughts of peace, and not of evil, to give you an expected end. (Jeremiah 29:11)

> To the praise of the glory of his grace, wherein he hath made us accepted in the beloved. (Ephesians 1:6)

HOW DOES GOD VIEW THE BELIEVER?

The "beloved" in view is the Lord Jesus Christ. The word we are focusing on is *accepted*, which may also be translated "to make lovely, endue with special honor, or to bestow grace upon." No matter how we feel, we are accepted by Christ because of his sacrifice. Isn't it marvelous how God made us accepted and never to be rejected? When the world rejects us for any reason, we know that we may come to Christ who will never reject us (Hebrews 13:5). Since we are accepted, we may come with confidence to the throne of grace (Hebrews 4:16) and speak whatever is on our heart. The unsaved cannot do this, because they are not accepted. Let us remember that it is with God we are going to spend eternity, so if the world rejects us, so what? Because this world is fleeting away, but the believers' lives are ready to flourish. So have courage, because you are accepted!

> In whom we have redemption through his blood,
> the forgiveness of sins, according to the riches of
> his grace; (Ephesians 1:7)

Redemption is another glorious word in this spiritual catalog. Redemption may also be translated "ransom in full, a buying back, deliverance from guilt and punishment from sin." Never will a believer have to stand in judgment for their sin because the work of Christ was complete on our behalf. We were totally redeemed from all sin and guilt. This applies to past, present, and future, because when Christ went to the cross, all your sins were in the future. Our redemption was secured by God himself, plus he declares us sinless. It would do good to read Romans 8:33 again. So let the accusers accuse, the mockers mock, the gossipers gossip, because God knows who his children are, and once he has declared them redeemed, it is forever.

The word *forgiveness* may also be translated "freedom, pardon, or release from sin." This word states the Christian has absolute pardon from all their sin. Since we have been totally forgiven, we are eternally secure, because God sees us as sinless. Being in Christ guarantees our place in heaven. We are totally free from all spiritual penalties owing to sin. However, there may be physical penalties for sin, such as AIDS for sexual sins or liver disease from drinking, and others which we previously saw. You can take comfort that even though our flesh is corrupting, the inner man is being renewed daily (2 Corinthians 4:16). This is why the believer radiates an inner joy, because all the baggage of sin has been removed permanently and figuratively cast behind God's back:

> Behold, for peace I had great bitterness: but thou hast in love to my soul delivered it from the pit of corruption: for thou hast cast all my sins behind thy back. (Isaiah 38:17)

This is why the believer is free to do the work of the Lord, because sin no longer impedes the believer. However, if there is a besetting sin in a believer's life, this may cause an impediment. A besetting sin will definitely be a hindrance to usefulness in God's kingdom. Just because someone has been placed on the shelf by God does not take away from the fact they are totally forgiven. Total forgiveness does not justify a believer for continuing in the life of sin; he/she must mortify the deeds of the flesh (Romans 8:13), and it will not be easy.

> In whom also we have obtained an inheritance, being predestinated according to the purpose of him who worketh all things after the counsel of his own will. (Ephesians 1:11)

The word *inheritance* may also be translated "to allot, to obtain, possess." The Christian is guaranteed to inherit heaven and all the spiritual blessings as we previously discovered. If our hope was only in this world, I would definitely be depressed, but because God is viewing us as his children, he has given us the greatest inheritance that we could ever ask for or dream of—*himself!* Genesis 15:1 states:

> After these things the word of the LORD came unto Abram in a vision, saying, Fear not, Abram:

> I am thy shield, and thy exceeding great reward.
> (Genesis 15:1)

The word *reward* may also be translated "pay or wages." The believer's wages will actually be God himself! Talk about an inheritance which is beyond comprehension! Compare these wages to the wages of sin in Romans 6:23:

> For the wages of sin is death; but the gift of God is eternal life through Jesus Christ our Lord.
> (Romans 6:23)

We have looked at only eight verses and saw the marvelous way which God views his children and how he has provided for us. No other group in the world is going to experience what you and I will. Don't just stop at these verses; as you grow in your biblical knowledge, you will be able to analyze all the promises of God, and as you do, you will become better acquainted with God. Before we leave this study, I wish to offer some Scriptures from both the Old and New Testaments, furthering our insight on how God views his redeemed children.

God Will Bless the Work of Our Hands

"And the LORD thy God will make thee plenteous in every work of thine hand, in the fruit of thy body, and in the fruit of thy cattle, and in the fruit of thy land, for good: for the LORD will again rejoice over thee for good, as he rejoiced over thy fathers" (Deuteronomy 30:9).

Lot of God's Inheritance

"For the LORD's portion is his people; Jacob is the lot of his inheritance" (Deuteronomy 32:9).

The Holy Hill

"A Psalm of David. LORD, who shall abide in thy tabernacle? who shall dwell in thy holy hill" (Psalm 15:1)?

The Lord Preserves His People

"For the LORD loveth judgment, and forsaketh not his saints; they are preserved for ever: but the seed of the wicked shall be cut off" (Psalm 37:28).

The Congregation of the Lord's Poor

"O deliver not the soul of thy turtledove unto the multitude of the wicked: forget not the congregation of thy poor forever" (Psalm 74:19).

The Assembly of the Saints

"God is greatly to be feared in the assembly of the saints, and to be had in reverence of all them that are about him" (Psalm 89:7).

The Assembly of the Upright

"Praise ye the LORD. I will praise the LORD with my whole heart, in the assembly of the upright, and in the congregation" (Psalm 111:1).

God Protects his People

"A Song of degrees. They that trust in the LORD shall be as mount Zion, which cannot be removed, but abideth forever. {2} As the mountains are round about Jerusalem, so the LORD is round about his people from henceforth even forever" (Psalm 125:1–2).

The Congregation of the Saints

"Praise ye the LORD. Sing unto the LORD a new song, and his praise in the congregation of saints" (Psalm 149:1).

The Mountain of the Lord's House

"And it shall come to pass in the last days, that the mountain of the Lord's house shall be established in the top of the mountains, and shall be exalted above the hills; and all nations shall flow unto it" (Isaiah 2:2).

God Will Gently Shepherd Us

"He shall feed his flock like a shepherd: he shall gather the lambs with his arm, and carry them in his bosom, and shall gently lead those that are with young" (Isaiah 40:11).

We Are His Witnesses in the World

"Ye are my witnesses, saith the LORD, and my servant whom I have chosen: that ye may know and believe me, and understand that I am he: before me there was no God formed, neither shall there be after me" (Isaiah 43:10).

The Branch of God's Planting

"Thy people also shall be all righteous: they shall inherit the land for ever, the branch of my planting, the work of my hands, that I may be glorified" (Isaiah 60:21).

Beulah

"Thou shalt no more be termed Forsaken; neither shall thy land any more be termed Desolate: but thou shalt be called Hephzibah, and thy land Beulah: for the LORD delighteth in thee, and thy land shall be married" (Isaiah 62:4).

Sought Out, A City Not Forsaken

"And they shall call them, The holy people, The redeemed of the LORD: and thou shalt be called, Sought out, A city not forsaken" (Isaiah 62:12).

A Pleasant Portion

"Many pastors have destroyed my vineyard, they have trodden my portion under foot, they have made my pleasant portion a desolate wilderness" (Jeremiah 12:10).

God Loves His Children Eternally

"The LORD hath appeared of old unto me, saying, Yea, I have loved thee with an everlasting love: therefore with lovingkindness have I drawn thee" (Jeremiah 31:3).

The Place of God's Throne

"And he said unto me, Son of man, the place of my throne, and the place of the soles of my feet, where I will dwell in the midst of the children of Israel forever, and my holy name, shall the house of Israel no more defile, neither they, nor their kings, by their whoredom, nor by the carcasses of their kings in their high places" (Ezekiel 43:7).

The City of Truth, the Mountain of the Lord, and the Holy Mountain

"Thus saith the LORD; I am returned unto Zion, and will dwell in the midst of Jerusalem: and Jerusalem shall be called a city of truth; and the mountain of the LORD of hosts the holy mountain" (Zechariah 8:3).

A Pearl of Great Price

"Again, the kingdom of heaven is like unto a merchant man, seeking goodly pearls: {46} Who, when he had found one pearl of great price, went and sold all that he had, and bought it" (Matthew 13:45–46).

The Vineyard

"They say unto him, he will miserably destroy those wicked men, and will let out his vineyard unto other husbandmen, which shall render him the fruits in their seasons" (Matthew 21:41).

Resurrection Hope

"And this is the Father's will which hath sent me, that of all which he hath given me I should lose nothing, but should raise it up again at the last day. {40} And this is the will of him that sent me, that everyone which seeth the Son, and believeth on him, may have everlasting life: and I will raise him up at the last day." (John 6:39–40).

The Fold of Christ

"And other sheep I have, which are not of this fold: them also I must bring, and they shall hear my voice; and there shall be one fold, and one shepherd" (John 10:16).

The Church of God

"Take heed therefore unto yourselves, and to all the flock, over the which the Holy Ghost hath made you overseers, to feed the church of God, which he hath purchased with his own blood" (Acts 20:28).

God is On Our Side

"What shall we then say to these things? If God be for us, who can be against us" (Romans 8:31)?

God is Our Justifier

"Who shall lay anything to the charge of God's elect? It is God that justifieth" (Romans 8:33).

We Are God's Tilled Field

"For we are labourers together with God: ye are God's husbandry, ye are God's building" (1 Corinthians 3:9).

We Are the Temple of the Living God

"And what agreement hath the temple of God with idols? for ye are the temple of the living God; as God hath said, I will dwell in them, and walk in them; and I will be their God, and they shall be my people" (2 Corinthians 6:16).

The Israel of God

"And as many as walk according to this rule, peace be on them, and mercy, and upon the Israel of God" (Galatians 6:16).

The Body of Christ

"And hath put all things under his feet, and gave him to be the head over all things to the church, {23} Which is his body, the fulness of him that filleth all in all" (Ephesians 1:22–23).

God Sees Us Reigning in Heaven Already

"And hath raised us up together, and made us sit together in heavenly places in Christ Jesus" (Ephesians 2:6).

We Are His Workmanship

"For we are his workmanship, created in Christ Jesus unto good works, which God hath before ordained that we should walk in them" (Ephesians 2:10).

The Family of Heaven and Earth

"Of whom the whole family in heaven and earth is named" (Ephesians 3:15).

We Are Reconciled unto God

"And you, that were sometime alienated and enemies in your mind by wicked works, yet now hath he reconciled" (Colossians 1:21).

Church of the Living God and Pillar and Ground of Truth

"But if I tarry long, that thou mayest know how thou oughtest to behave thyself in the house of God, which is the church of the living God, the pillar and ground of the truth" (1 Timothy 3:15).

City of the Living God and Mount Zion

"But ye are come unto mount Sion, and unto the city of the living God, the heavenly Jerusalem, and to an innumerable company of angels" (Hebrews 12:22).

Church of the Firstborn

"To the general assembly and church of the firstborn, which are written in heaven, and to God the Judge of all, and to the spirits of just men made perfect" (Hebrews 12:23).

We Have a Reserved Inheritance

"Blessed be the God and Father of our Lord Jesus Christ, which according to his abundant mercy hath begotten us again unto a lively hope by the resurrection of Jesus Christ from the dead, {4} To an inheritance incorruptible, and undefiled, and that fadeth not away, reserved in heaven for you" (1 Peter 1:3–4).

Chosen, Holy, and Royal People

"But ye are a chosen generation, a royal priesthood, an holy nation, a peculiar people; that ye should show forth the praises of him who hath called you out of darkness into his marvelous light" (1 Peter 2:9).

The Flock of God

"Feed the flock of God which is among you, taking the oversight thereof, not by constraint, but willingly; not for filthy lucre, but of a ready mind" (1 Peter 5:2).

The Sons/Daughters of the Living God

"Beloved, now are we the sons of God, and it doth not yet appear what we shall be: but we know that, when he shall appear, we shall be like him; for we shall see him as he is" (1 John 3:2).

The Heavenly Jerusalem

"Him that overcometh will I make a pillar in the temple of my God, and he shall go no more out: and I will write upon him the name of my God, and the name of the city of my God, which is new Jerusalem, which cometh down out of heaven from my God: and I will write upon him my new name" (Revelation 3:12).

The Holy City

"And I John saw the holy city, new Jerusalem, coming down from God out of heaven, prepared as a bride adorned for her husband" (Revelation 21:2).

The Bride of Christ

"And there came unto me one of the seven angels which had the seven vials full of the seven last plagues, and talked with me, saying, Come hither, I will show thee the bride, the Lamb's wife" (Revelation 21:9).

Prophecy

The word *prophecy* means a foretelling of the future or a declaration of something to come. The Bible has much to say about prophecy. The earthly ministry of the Lord Jesus Christ was prophesied way back in Genesis 3:15. True biblical prophecy must always be from the Scriptures and not from outside sources. The type of prophecy we have today coming from many Christian ministries are actually false teachings, and we will look at some of these teachings.

It seems there is a fascination among many Christians concerning the return of the Lord Jesus Christ. Jesus did say that he would return for his church, and that day has already been set as we read in Acts 17:31.

> Because he hath appointed a day, in the which he will judge the world in righteousness by that man whom he hath ordained; whereof he hath given assurance unto all men, in that he hath raised him from the dead. (Acts 17:31)

The problem is not that Christians desire to see the Lord return, but it is the methods that many employ to predict the date of his return.

Some use dates such as the founding of modern Israel in 1948, plus they add forty or seventy years to it because they claim that these are the lengths of generations found in the Bible. Some try to use numerology based upon the numbers found in the Bible. Some have tried to use the feasts of Israel as found in Leviticus and other places.

We will look at the fallacy of date setting to show how ungodly this practice is.

When I was a new Christian, my biggest mistake was that I started out by purchasing many prophecy books, and as many books as there were, there were just as many opinions which caused confusion in my understanding of the Bible in this area. God has made it very easy for us to understand prophetic things if we stick to the Scriptures alone, because they are sufficient to give us understanding in this area.

Here is a quote by Charles Haddon Spurgeon who was a preacher in England in the second half of the nineteenth century.

> In many cases sheer fanaticism has been the result of exclusively dwelling on prophecy, and probably more men have gone mad on that subject than on any other religious questions.

Many cult leaders claim they were the fulfillment of prophecy such as David Koresh, Father Divine, Sun Myung Moon, and others, because they wrongly interpreted the Bible by twisting Scripture. Back in January 2018, there was a man in Russia who claimed to be the incarnation of Christ and had amassed 5,000 followers.

The obsession that people have with Bible prophecy is beyond normal and must be controlled. The Lord will return on the day he has already chosen and not one day before or one day after. The reason that prophecy preachers are wrong in their estimations is because they interpret the Bible according to newspapers, news broadcasts, daily happenings, magazines, archaeology, etc. True Bible prophecy can only come about when we interpret the Scriptures by the Scriptures.

Date Setters

One of the worst groups both within and outside Christianity are those who think they have figured out when the Lord will return. I have included a list I compiled concerning the dates, and the date setters which you can see have all been 100 percent wrong; and the way we can tell they were wrong is that we are still here. You will also see that there are some solid Christians who partook of this error such as Martin Luther and Cotton Mather. Date setters bring much mockery to Christianity. For example, Harold Camping, the late president of Family Radio in Oakland, California, predicted the world would end in both 1994 and May 21, 2011. This 2011 prediction received worldwide attention, because many of his followers went to different countries and preached this lie.

Here is a case of a follower of this prophecy who made a complete fool of himself in front of many people, plus it was televised. A man who followed Camping's prediction was standing in Times Square in New York City and was preaching to people that the end had come and it would come at 6:00 p.m. on May 21 when he would be raptured in front of them. Well 6:00 came and went, and nothing happened. The man was mocked for his mindless behavior. This is what happens when we try and know more than what the Bible reveals to us.

> But of that day and hour knoweth no man, no, not the angels of heaven, but my Father only. (Matthew 24:36)

80 AD—Ben Zakkai died about 80, and expected the Messiah about the time of his death.
331 AD—Tichonus writer of the fourth century.
470 AD—Rabbi Hanina.
500 AD—Hippolytus (170–236) and Iranaeus (130–202) Both based Prediction on measurement of the Ark. Lactantius (250–330).
1000 AD—Hysteria reigned at this magical date.
1009 AD—Rain of blood; sun turns red and fails to shine for three days; plague and death follow.
1147 AD—Gerard of Poehlde decided that the millennium had actually started in 306 AD during Constantine's reign and the world end would happen in 1306 AD.

PROPHECY

1186 AD—John of Toledo.
1533 AD—Melchior Hoffman.
1600 AD—Martin Luther.
1656 AD—Christopher Columbus.
1689 AD—Benjamin Keach.
1697 AD—Cotton Mather—Also predicted 1716 and 1736.
1715 AD—William Whiston.
1794 AD—Charles Wesley.
1844 AD—William Miller (Seventh Day Adventists).
1859 AD—Rev. Thomas Parker expected the Millennium to begin.
1874 AD—Jehovah's Witnesses.
1910 AD—Charles Taze Russell.
1914 AD—Jehovah's Witnesses.
1915 AD—Jehovah's Witnesses.
1929 AD—Jehovah's Witnesses.
1943 AD—Herbert W. Armstrong.
1953 AD—David Davidson—In his book, *The Great Pyramid, Its Divine Message.*
1970 AD—True Light Church of Christ.
1977 AD—William Branham.
1979 AD—Walter M. Simmons.
1981 AD—Bill Maupin and the Lighthouse Gospel Tract Foundation.
1981 AD—Hal Lindsey.
1982 AD—Benjamin Creme.
1988 AD—Edgar Whisenant.
1988 AD—J. R. Church (Hidden Prophecies in the Psalms) I heard this one with my own ears in 1983 in Oklahoma City.
1989 AD—Edgar Whisenant.
1992 AD—Korean group called Mission for the coming days.
1994 AD—Pastor John Hinkle.
1994 AD—Harold Camping (When it did not happen he changed his story and claimed the Church was being judged by Christ—Same as Seventh Day Adventists)
1995 AD—Harold Camping.
1996 AD—Harold Camping.

1998 AD—Heng Ming-Chen, leader of Taiwanese cult out of Garland, Texas.
1999 AD—Kirk Nelson.
1999 AD—Mone Kim Miller (Concerned Christians).
1999 AD—Nostradamus (1503–1566).
2000 AD—Isaac Newton (1643–1727).
2000 AD—Lester Sumrall.
2000 AD—Tom Holt (Editor of *Family Radio Digest*).
2001 AD—Charles Spiegel.
2001 AD—Dan Millar.
2004 AD—Arnie Stanton.
2007 AD—Hal Lindsey.
2007 AD—Shelby Corbett (She placed signs on benches).
2008 AD—Marilyn Agee.
2008 AD—Ronald Weinland.
2011 AD—Harold Camping (he has also named the day May 21 for the rapture and October 21 for the annihilation of the unsaved).
2011 AD—Paul Aarons (May 21).
2012 AD—The Mayan Calendar ends on December 21.
2015 AD—E Bible Fellowship (Chris McCann named October 7).
2017 AD—David Meade (September 23; October 15)
2018 AD—(May 20) Patrick Cody (Hyper-Campingite).
2018 AD—Jack Van Impe.
2034 AD—John Denton (Bible Research and Investigation Company).

Rapture

The Rapture is the event in history when the Lord Jesus Christ is going to return to earth and rapture all of the saved. 1 Thessalonians 4:13–18 records this event. The question is not whether there is a rapture but when it will occur. The prevalent teaching is that it will happen before a "seven-year tribulation period," which begins ushering in the final years of earth's history. This comes from the dispensational point of view which is a man-made system of beliefs. Once again, once we let the Bible tell us when the rapture is, all other guesses will be insignificant. The Bible is very clear that the rapture will be on the last day. The Bible gives us many Scripture verses, telling us that it is on the last day, which is the last day of recorded history.

Matthew 13:24–30 to Matthew 13:39–40—Harvest is end of the world.
Matthew 13:47–49—Harvest is the end of the world.
John 5:28–29—One general resurrection of both the saved and unsaved.
John 6:39—Last day.
John 6:40—Last day.
John 6:54—Last day.
John 11:24—Last day.
John 12:48—Last day.
1 Corinthians 15:51–53—The last trump.

> 24 Another parable put he forth unto them, saying, The kingdom of heaven is likened unto a man which sowed good seed in his field: 25 But while men slept, his enemy came and sowed tares among the wheat, and went his way. 26 But when the blade was sprung up, and brought forth fruit, then appeared the tares also. 27 So the servants of the householder came and said unto him, Sir, didst not thou sow good seed in thy field? from whence then hath it tares? 28 he said unto them, An enemy hath done this. The servants said unto him, Wilt thou then that we go and gather them up? 29 But he said, Nay; lest while ye gather up the tares, ye root up also the wheat with them. 30 Let both grow together until the harvest: and in the time of harvest I will say to the reapers, Gather ye together first the tares, and bind them in bundles to burn them: but gather the wheat into my barn. (Matthew 13:24–30)

39 The enemy that sowed them is the devil; the harvest is the end of the world; and the reapers are the angels. 40 As therefore the tares are gathered and burned in the fire; so shall it be in the end of this world. (Matthew 13:39–40)

47 Again, the kingdom of heaven is like unto a net, that was cast into the sea, and gathered of every kind: 48 Which, when it was full, they drew to shore, and sat down, and gathered the good into vessels, but cast the bad away. 49 So shall it be at the end of the world: the angels shall come forth, and sever the wicked from among the just, (Matthew 13:47–49)

28 Marvel not at this: for the hour is coming, in the which all that are in the graves shall hear his voice, 29 And shall come forth; they that have done good, unto the resurrection of life; and they that have done evil, unto the resurrection of damnation. (John 5:28–29)

And this is the Father's will which hath sent me, that of all which he hath given me I should lose nothing, but should raise it up again at the last day. (John 6:39)

And this is the will of him that sent me, that everyone which seeth the Son, and believeth on him, may have everlasting life: and I will raise him up at the last day. (John 6:40)

Whoso eateth my flesh, and drinketh my blood, hath eternal life; and I will raise him up at the last day. (John 6:54)

> Martha saith unto him, I know that he shall rise again in the resurrection at the last day. (John 11:24)

> He that rejecteth me, and receiveth not my words, hath one that judgeth him: the word that I have spoken, the same shall judge him in the last day. (John 12:48)

> 51 Behold, I shew you a mystery; We shall not all sleep, but we shall all be changed, 52 In a moment, in the twinkling of an eye, at the last trump: for the trumpet shall sound, and the dead shall be raised incorruptible, and we shall be changed. 53 For this corruptible must put on incorruption, and this mortal must put on immortality. (1 Corinthians 15:51–53)

When we look at these Scripture verses, can it be any clearer as to the timing of the Rapture? God is telling us that it will occur on the last day, and until that time, we are to be occupied with sending forth the Gospel to the world.

> And he called his ten servants, and delivered them ten pounds, and said unto them, Occupy till I come. (Luke 19:13 KJV)

Millennium

There is another teaching which is prevalent among the majority of churches, and that is the teaching on the "millennium." The millennium is a period of 1,000 years when the Lord Jesus Christ will return to earth and set up an earthly kingdom. This teaching is another aspect of Dispensationalism and is not found in Scripture but is a manufactured belief based upon the erroneous understanding of Revelation 20.

> 4 And I saw thrones, and they sat upon them, and judgment was given unto them: and I saw the souls of them that were beheaded for the witness of Jesus, and for the word of God, and which had not worshipped the beast, neither his image, neither had received his mark upon their foreheads, or in their hands; and they lived and reigned with Christ a thousand years. 5 But the rest of the dead lived not again until the thousand years were finished. This is the first resurrection. 6 Blessed and holy is he that hath part in the first resurrection: on such the second death hath no power, but they shall be priests of God and of Christ, and shall reign with him a thousand years. 7 And when the thousand years are expired, Satan shall be loosed out of his prison, (Revelation 20:4–7)

As you can see, if we were to take literally these verses in Revelation 20, we would see the term "thousand years" is used four times. So if one listens to a preacher of Dispensationalism, they will be convinced that Christ is going to reign one thousand years, and that reign will take place in Jerusalem. However, when we search the Scriptures, we find an interesting phrase in many of them which is "last days." My question is this: if we are in the last days, how can there be another thousand years following? Then shouldn't those be the last days? Let us look at a few of those Scriptures which refute the idea of a coming millennium.

> 29 Immediately after the tribulation of those days shall the sun be darkened, and the moon shall not give her light, and the stars shall fall from heaven, and the powers of the heavens shall be shaken: 30 And then shall appear the sign of the Son of man in heaven: and then shall all the tribes of the earth mourn, and they shall see the

> Son of man coming in the clouds of heaven with
> power and great glory. (Matthew 24:29–30)

In Matthew 24:29–30, we read some interesting information. First it states that "immediately after the tribulation of those days," the universe is starting to collapse right on the last day, so how do you fit 1,000 years into verse 29, especially with the word *immediately*?

Secondly, the Lord Jesus Christ is returning right on the heels of that collapse. Genesis 1:14 gives us insight as to why we were given the sun, moon, and stars.

> And God said, Let there be lights in the firmament of the heaven to divide the day from the night; and let them be for signs, and for seasons, and for days, and years. (Genesis 1:14)

Verse 30 speaks of the sign of the Son of man, and Genesis 1:14 speaks of the universe being given as a sign. The sign is simple—the universe is collapsing at the same time the Lord returns for his people. Remember in the last section on the Rapture, we read in John 5:28–29 that there will be one general resurrection on one day? And here it is: the Lord returns one time for his people and to judge the unbeliever.

> And it shall come to pass in the last days, that the mountain of the LORD'S house shall be established in the top of the mountains, and shall be exalted above the hills; and all nations shall flow unto it. (Isaiah 2:2)

> But in the last days it shall come to pass, that the mountain of the house of the LORD shall be established in the top of the mountains, and it shall be exalted above the hills; and people shall flow unto it. (Micah 4:1)

And it shall come to pass in the last days, saith God, I will pour out of my Spirit upon all flesh: and your sons and your daughters shall prophesy, and your young men shall see visions, and your old men shall dream dreams: (Acts 2:17)

This know also, that in the last days perilous times shall come. (2 Tim 3:1)

1 God, who at sundry times and in diverse manners spake in time past unto the fathers by the prophets, 2 Hath in these last days spoken unto us by his Son, whom he hath appointed heir of all things, by whom also he made the worlds; (Hebrews 1:1–2)

Your gold and silver is cankered; and the rust of them shall be a witness against you, and shall eat your flesh as it were fire. Ye have heaped treasure together for the last days. (James 5:3)

Who are kept by the power of God through faith unto salvation ready to be revealed in the last time. (1 Pet. 1:5)

Who verily was foreordained before the foundation of the world, but was manifest in these last times for you, (1 Pet. 1:20)

Knowing this first, that there shall come in the last days scoffers, walking after their own lusts, (2 Pet. 3:3)

Little children, it is the last time: and as ye have heard that antichrist shall come, even now are

there many antichrists; whereby we know that it
is the last time. (1 John 2:18)

How that they told you there should be mockers
in the last time, who should walk after their own
ungodly lusts. (Jude 1:18)

We have just listed twelve verses which all reference the fact that we are living in the last days. So if we are living in the last days, there is no way there can be another set of last days. If I am down to my last dollar and I spend it, there is no more money left. If I have one dollar and I spend it, but I have one thousand dollars in my pocket, then I am not down to my last dollar. I have written an article on the millennium which is available online for free use at www.scionofzion.com/millennium.htm.

Israel

There is another teaching which has basically permeated the majority of churches, and that is the erroneous belief that the modern nation of Israel is a fulfillment of prophecy. Ancient Israel had a special relationship with God, because through the tribe of Judah came the Lord Jesus Christ. The modern nation of Israel is just one nation among all the nations of the world and holds no special relationship to God since they are in rebellion to God because of their ongoing hatred of the Lord Jesus Christ.

When Christ went to the cross, many things had changed, and that included the fact that the terms which described ancient Israel were now being applied to the eternal church. Between the years of 66–74 AD, the ancient nation of Israel was dissolved by means of the Roman army decimating it. Many of the Jews were taken to Rome as slaves and many were killed trying to defend their homeland, but it was to no avail. The final straw in their rebellion against God was when they betrayed Christ into the hands of the Romans and then called for his execution.

As you read the Old Testament, you will read many places where God sent judgments against them for their disobedience, but I want to include a few verses which shows that definition changed after the cross.

> 28 For he is not a Jew, which is one outwardly; neither is that circumcision, which is outward in the flesh: 29 But he is a Jew, which is one inwardly; and circumcision is that of the heart, in the spirit, and not in the letter; whose praise is not of men, but of God. (Romans 2:28–29)

> 2 Beware of dogs, beware of evil workers, beware of the concision. 3 For we are the circumcision, which worship God in the spirit, and rejoice in Christ Jesus, and have no confidence in the flesh. (Philippians 3:2–3)

> Not as though the word of God hath taken none effect. For they are not all Israel, which are of Israel: (Romans 9:6)

> And as many as walk according to this rule, peace be on them, and mercy, and upon the Israel of God. (Galatians 6:16)

> Circumcise therefore the foreskin of your heart, and be no more stiff-necked. (Deuteronomy 10:16)

> And the LORD thy God will circumcise thine heart, and the heart of thy seed, to love the LORD thy God with all thine heart, and with all thy soul, that thou mayest live. (Deuteronomy 30:6)

PROPHECY

Even back in the time of Moses which was about 1447 BC, we read that the Scriptures were already looking forward to the time when the Lord Jesus Christ would come on the scene to save his people. Notice in Deuteronomy 10:16, we read that Israel was to circumcise its heart; and then further in 30:6, it states that God will circumcise the heart; and then in Romans 2:29, it states plainly that circumcision is of the heart. These are all words of salvation; "circumcision of the heart" means God gives a new heart.

> 26 A new heart also will I give you, and a new spirit will I put within you: and I will take away the stony heart out of your flesh, and I will give you an heart of flesh. 27 And I will put my spirit within you, and cause you to walk in my statutes, and ye shall keep my judgments, and do them. (Ezekiel 36:26–27)

In Ezekiel 36:26–27, we read that God is going to give a new spirit and a new heart. Both of these are pointing to the grace of God in salvation.

In the first covenant, God required circumcision to show that you were in covenant with him, but in the second covenant which is the covenant of grace, the circumcision is of the heart, which means that God saves you and places the Holy Spirit within you, giving you a new heart and new spirit. God is doing this all over the world as his means of salvation.

Since the Hebrew Scriptures were looking forward to the Lord Jesus Christ and the covenant of grace, there would be no reason for a second Israel to be built. The Israel of God in the New Testament is the eternal church of God as the Apostle Paul stated in Galatians 6:16 above. The modern nation of Israel has become a literal idol in the majority of churches, and God forbids idolatry. There is not one mention of another political Israel in the entire New Testament. If God was going to reform another nation of Israel like ancient Israel, you would think that he would have at least mentioned it once in the New Testament.

For further information on Israel, I have written an article which may be used freely entitled "The Israel of God" at www.scionofzion.com/israelofgod.htm.

Antichrist

I remember when I was a new Christian, and the Bible was something new and exciting. I followed the advice of Bible teachers that I should purchase some books which would help me gain a better understanding of Scripture. Being a new Christian, I latched onto the prophecy craze which is still going strong today. I purchased books by many different authors.

One thing they all had in common was their desire to identify the Antichrist. I remember being in Oklahoma City in 1983 for a prophecy meeting with Southwest Radio Church, and a preacher gave a multimedia presentation on how he believed the Antichrist would appear.

These pre-tribulation theologians look everywhere for the revealing of the Antichrist, except in the Bible. When God first accepted me by his sovereign will, I too fell into the trap of trying to identify the Antichrist. In 1981, we were looking at the possibility of David Rockefeller being the Antichrist. Then we thought it was Ronald Wilson Reagan (three names of six letters, each 666); then Gorbachev came on the scene, and we thought it might be him (some even thought his patch of discolored skin on his head might be the mark of the beast).

In July of 1994, a new candidate for Antichrist came on the scene from Russia; his name was Zhirinovsky. This happened because I was interpreting the Bible by politics and news reports. Once I did away with the method of Bible interpretation by newspapers and studied the Scriptures on the matter, it became clear who the Antichrist was.

The standard belief is that there is going to rise up a man who will be indwelled by Satan and will rule the world for a period of seven years until he is destroyed at the return of the Lord Jesus Christ. Let me say at the outset that the Antichrist is Satan, because he is the only one who fits the description fully. We will focus on the term *man*, but it will not take on the same meaning we are used to for this instance only.

> Let no man deceive you by any means: for that day shall not come, except there come a falling away first, and that man of sin be revealed, the son of perdition. (2 Thessalonians 2:3)

> 12 How art thou fallen from heaven, O Lucifer, son of the morning! how art thou cut down to the ground, which didst weaken the nations! 13 For thou hast said in thine heart, I will ascend into heaven, I will exalt my throne above the stars of God: I will sit also upon the mount of the congregation, in the sides of the north: 14 I will ascend above the heights of the clouds; I will be like the most High. 15 Yet thou shalt be brought down to hell, to the sides of the pit. 16 They that see thee shall narrowly look upon thee, and consider thee, saying, Is this the man that made the earth to tremble, that did shake kingdoms; 17 That made the world as a wilderness, and destroyed the cities thereof; that opened not the house of his prisoners? (Isaiah 14:12–17)

I wanted to include the entire passage so the context would be included and we can see that in no uncertain terms how the Bible uses the term *man* to describe Satan. Notice in 2 Thessalonians 2:3, it speaks about "that man of sin" who will be revealed. Then we look at Isaiah 14:12–17 and we focus in on verse 16 where it states "Is this the man that made the earth to tremble." If we stopped there, then there is a possibility that it could be a physical man, but we don't stop there. Notice in verse 17 how it speaks about not opening the house of his prisoners. When Jesus came on the scene, he spoke a passage from Isaiah, and in the passage, it spoke about captives.

> The Spirit of the Lord is upon me, because he hath anointed me to preach the gospel to the poor; he hath sent me to heal the brokenhearted, to preach deliverance to the captives, and recovering of sight to the blind, to set at liberty them that are bruised, (Luke 4:18)

Notice that he came to preach deliverance to the captives; that is, he is going to bring the gospel to those that are captive in Satan's house which is a prison of sin and death, and when they become saved, they will come forth in freedom from Satan's prison. Now I want to refocus on "man." Satan is referred to as a man in 2 Thessalonians 2:3 and in Isaiah 14:16, and we know from the study of the Scriptures that Satan is a spirit, a fallen angel, and does not have a physical body.

One more Scripture verse.

> Who is a liar but he that denieth that Jesus is the Christ? he is antichrist, that denieth the Father and the Son. (1 John 2:22)

Many groups around the world deny that Jesus is the Christ or Savior. They are also referred to as Antichrist. The word *antichrist* in the Greek can also be translated "against Christ," and there are many who are against Christ. The word *is* is in the present tense in the Greek, which means that Antichrist was around 2,000 years ago and is around today, and only Satan fills that time length.

Now human beings that deny Christ are only doing so because in their fallen, spiritually dead state, they believe false teachings which are given by Satan to his loyal followers. So in essence, Satan the ultimate Antichrist and fuels his human antichrists with false teachings. I have written an article on the Antichrist which is available for free usage at www.scionofzion.com/antichrist.htm.

Rewards

There is another teaching which is prevalent in many churches, and that is the idea of receiving rewards for living a faithful and involved life. Many preachers and evangelists love the idea of rewards, because they believe that because of their positions, they will receive great rewards when the Lord returns on the last day. The concept of receiving special rewards for service is foreign to the Scriptures and is another belief which was superimposed upon the Scriptures.

> So likewise ye, when ye shall have done all those things which are commanded you, say, We are unprofitable servants: we have done that which was our duty to do. (Luke 17:10)

When we read a verse like Luke 17:10, it quashes the idea of somehow being rewarded to do what we are saved and commanded to do. We forget that we were once dead sinners in rebellion against God, and it was God who saved us and took us out of the kingdom of Satan. The idea of rewards is an idea based in pride that somehow God owes us more than he has given us. Read the following verses:

> 29 And he said unto them, Verily I say unto you, There is no man that hath left house, or parents, or brethren, or wife, or children, for the kingdom of God's sake, 30 Who shall not receive manifold more in this present time, and in the world to come life everlasting. (Luke 18:29–30)

Notice where God has placed the blessings. The Lord Jesus Christ states that any blessings given in the Christian life will be given in this world. Then Jesus goes on to say that those who are faithful in this life, for the kingdom's sake, will receive life everlasting in the world to come. In the new heavens and new earth, what need will there be for extra rewards? Look at Genesis 15:1:

> After these things the word of the LORD came unto Abram in a vision, saying, Fear not, Abram: I am thy shield, and thy exceeding great reward. (Genesis 15:1)

God told Abram that he was Abram's exceeding great reward. God himself is the reward of the believer. Let us look at some verses which use the word *reward* in it, and we will see if faithful Christians will receive special rewards.

> 17 For if I do this thing willingly, I have a reward: but if against my will, a dispensation of the gospel is committed unto me. 18 What is my reward then? Verily that, when I preach the gospel, I may make the gospel of Christ without charge, that I abuse not my power in the gospel. (1 Corinthians 9:17–18)

Verse 17—Many people will volunteer for something if they believe they will receive some type of reward for their efforts. Paul is saying the same thing that if he chose to preach the Gospel, then he would have some type of reward. Yet, when the life of the Apostle Paul is examined, we see that his life was filled with much opposition. On one hand, he desires with all his heart to preach the Gospel; but on the other hand as a Jew, the teaching of the Gospel of Christ was anathema, so when he was called, it would have been against his will. In fact, every Christian who is called to preach will have both types of relationships with their ministry. They will desire to preach the Gospel, but when opposition arises and they want to head for cover, then they must realize they have been commissioned to preach, and hiding is not an option.

Paul is saying here that even if he doesn't want to preach the Gospel, he will have to anyway, because the Lord Jesus Christ has commissioned him to do so, and whether he likes it or not, he is commanded to do it. There are probably countless numbers of Christians who were initially called into the ministry and then refused to go. Then as God began to tighten the ropes around them, they found great release when they finally yielded to God's irreversible calling and went into the ministry that God commissioned them to. In other words, if God is calling you into ministry, you are not going to run the other way. Remember Jonah!

Verse 18—Paul then goes on to explain the reward he receives. He rejoices in the fact that he can bring the Gospel without requesting any funds to do so, which means that he is not abusing his power. Basically, what he is saying is that he can bring the Gospel with pure motives. He also does not have to be concerned with the anxious thoughts of something like, "How much are they going to give me or will it be enough to live on?"

Paul makes what he knows he needs, and that frees him up to bring the Gospel without any shackles on it in the area of money. This is what we need to adopt as our ministry philosophy. It is a very erroneous practice to sell CDs of sermons in churches. That should be a ministry of the church. The essence of ministry is to bring the Gospel free of charge.

One of the definitions of *minister* is to give aid or service. Can you imagine a poor person going into a ministry-sponsored clinic and being told they have to pay for medicine? Then how is that ministry? It then becomes a business. Can you imagine a missionary going to a foreign country and handing out tracts to the people but charging them for it? Ridiculous, isn't it? Yet, churches do this as a regular practice. They take up a collection each Sunday which should be used for ministry; instead, it is socked away and the Gospel is sold.

If churches would abandon this practice and give away the Gospel, there will be no lack of funding in that ministry.

> 13 Every man's work shall be made manifest: for the day shall declare it, because it shall be revealed by fire; and the fire shall try every man's work of what sort it is. 14 If any man's work abide which

> he hath built thereupon, he shall receive a reward.
> (1 Corinthians 3:13–14)

Verse 13—When wood, hay, and stubble are touched by fire, they are instantly consumed; but when gold, silver, and precious stones are touched by fire, they become purified. The work being tested here is that of the believer. Fire always represents judgment. The true believer brings the Gospel, but not all those bring the Gospel to become saved. Therefore, the fires of judgment shall test the works or the ones being witnessed to, and if they remain unsaved, then they will face the fire of judgment on the last day.

Well, on the last day, the works of that believer will be tried; that is, those who received the knowledge of the Gospel and remained unsaved will be judged and sent to eternal damnation. Therefore, the works of that believer in sowing will have been a loss. The believer's faithfulness for sending out the Gospel is not on trial; it is the results that it produced which will be on trial. This will take place at the Great White Throne Judgment.

Verse 14—Now what work will endure or abide? It is the finished work of the Lord Jesus Christ on Calvary. Remember how Paul told us to build on the foundation of the Lord Jesus Christ (1 Corinthians 3:11)? In Acts, we read that there is no other name whereby you can obtain salvation from (Acts 4:12). The abiding work here are those whom God had saved through the ministry of a Saint.

Now it speaks of a reward or "payment or wages." What is the reward that we receive? Let us go back to the parable of the sower (Matthew 13:3–8). Do you remember what happened when the seed fell on good ground, which typifies the elect? Those that became saved produced fruit of thirty, sixty, or one hundred fold. The reward of the sower is to share in the ministry of those producing the thirty, sixty, and one hundred fold. Now is this principle revealed any place else in the Bible? The answer is yes!

> Then Peter began to say unto him, Lo, we have left all, and have followed thee. {29} And Jesus answered and said, Verily I say unto you, There

PROPHECY

> is no man that hath left house, or brethren, or sisters, or father, or mother, or wife, or children, or lands, for my sake, and the gospel's, {30} But he shall receive an hundredfold now in this time, houses, and brethren, and sisters, and mothers, and children, and lands, with persecutions; and in the world to come eternal life. (Mark 10:28–30)

Do you notice what is revealed in this verse? Look at verse 30—all the rewards and material goods will be given in "this time" and in the world to come eternal life. The reward is we may get to see some of that fruit that we helped to reap in this life, but the next life is eternal life. Eternal life is the reward, payment, or wage of the believer! It is not crowns or a special place in heaven or special honors. After our work is complete, the wages God gives his children is eternal life. Isn't that enough?

> Knowing that of the Lord ye shall receive the reward of the inheritance: for ye serve the Lord Christ. (Colossians 3:24, KJV)

Here is where Paul is stating that the saved slave will receive their reward. On earth, a slave was the lowest social class, and it was totally rare that they would receive any tangible recompense for their service. Paul is encouraging them that since they are serving the Lord Jesus Christ, they too will receive that reward of the inheritance.

> 3 Blessed be the God and Father of our Lord Jesus Christ, which according to his abundant mercy hath begotten us again unto a lively hope by the resurrection of Jesus Christ from the dead, {4} To an inheritance incorruptible, and undefiled, and that fadeth not away, reserved in heaven for you, (1 Peter 1:3–4)

When we look at what the inheritance is, we see that it is the inheritance of heaven. No longer would the slave be a slave, but instead, they would be kings and priests in the kingdom of God.

> And hath made us kings and priests unto God and his Father; to him be glory and dominion for ever and ever. Amen. (Revelation 1:6)

Revelation 1:6 makes this abundantly clear. On earth, the Christian who works for a living or was a slave to a master would receive very little or no compensation; but in heaven, all of that will change, and that is why Paul wants them to keep their eye focused on Christ, because he is the one who gives out the true reward, which is eternal life.

> And he said unto them, Verily I say unto you, There is no man that hath left house, or parents, or brethren, or wife, or children, for the kingdom of God's sake, {30} Who shall not receive manifold more in this present time, and in the world to come life everlasting. (Luke 18:29–30)

> Esteeming the reproach of Christ greater riches than the treasures in Egypt: for he had respect unto the recompence of the reward. (Hebrews 11:26, KJV)

The question that should be asked is, where did Moses get all this understanding from? He was in the palace of Pharaoh, surrounded by idols and all kinds of temptations of this world, and I seriously doubt there were any Bible teachers in the palace of Pharaoh, especially since there was no Bible written yet. Allow me to offer a theory as to where Moses received the beginning of understanding. When he was given back to his mother by the daughter of Pharaoh, I believe that is when his biblical training began.

> Then said his sister to Pharaoh's daughter, Shall I go and call to thee a nurse of the Hebrew

women, that she may nurse the child for thee? {8} And Pharaoh's daughter said to her, Go. And the maid went and called the child's mother. {9} And Pharaoh's daughter said unto her, Take this child away, and nurse it for me, and I will give *thee* thy wages. And the woman took the child, and nursed it. {10} And the child grew, and she brought him unto Pharaoh's daughter, and he became her son. And she called his name Moses: and she said, Because I drew him out of the water. (Exodus 2:7–10)

If you notice in verse 10, it states that "the child grew," which means he was given back to the daughter of Pharaoh when he was beyond the age of being a baby. It is almost a sure thing that Jochebed had taught Moses all about the patriarchs and the promise of God, including the promise that God would deliver the nation of Israel from bondage. So Moses had all these things taught to him, and sometime in the future, when he became born again in Christ, he remembered these things, because the Holy Spirit had brought them to mind while he was being taught the truth about fleeting riches.

Moses was born again, because what else could possibly make a person turn their back on the world, especially the massive amount of riches at his disposal? The only thing that could cause a person to do that is to be born again and to seek the Lord and reject the things of this world. He considered that the reproach of Christ was a far better thing than the fleeting riches of Egypt. He fixed his eyes on the reward, which is not earthly, but heaven itself. Heaven is the reward for all true believers in Christ. A person who is unsaved is not going to turn his back on the wealth of Egypt. Only a saved person, indwelled by the Holy Spirit, will have the ability to assess objectively which is greater—the riches of earth or eternal life in heaven with God. Those in Christ will choose the latter, because they have been born again and see beyond the horizon of this earth and all its snares.

> I press toward the mark for the prize [award] of the high calling of God in Christ Jesus. (Philippians 3:14)

The reason we are not to bask in our past life is because we are to press toward the mark for the prize of our high calling in Christ by God. The word for *prize* in the Greek may also be understood as *award*. We see in this verse that the award is the high calling in Christ and not some special reward. In Latin, it is called the *summa citatio*, which is the "highest calling."

Just to summarize this section, the believer does not receive any special rewards for faithful service. Our reward is God himself and eternal life in Christ. We have the opposite of eternal life in Christ in the section on eternal damnation. Based on the fact the believer does not have to spend an eternity in the lake of fire, but in bliss for eternity, constitutes the greatest reward.

Tribulation Period

There is another false teaching that permeates many churches, and that is the idea of a seven-year tribulation period. It is supposed to be the time when the "physical antichrist" will come on the scene and rule the world from Israel. The first three and one half years is supposed to be a time of great peace in this world, which is a deception, but the second three and half years is supposed to be a time of great tribulation and affliction for the Christians and the Jewish people.

This belief was based upon a verse found in the book of Daniel. It is Daniel 9:27:

> And he shall confirm the covenant with many for one week: and in the midst of the week he shall cause the sacrifice and the oblation to cease, and

> for the overspreading of abominations he shall make it desolate, even until the consummation, and that determined shall be poured upon the desolate. (Daniel 9:27)

Daniel 9 contains the section of Scripture known as the Seventy Weeks of Daniel 9. In 9:27, it speaks about the seventieth week, but this week is interrupted right in the middle.

Now the seventieth week stands alone. Now we have to ask which covenant is in view? Is it the covenant of law or the covenant of grace? When we look at the term *many*, it is associated with the covenant of grace.

> So Christ was once offered to bear the sins of many; and unto them that look for him shall he appear the second time without sin unto salvation. (Hebrews 9:28)

Even in Daniel 12:2, it mentions the word *many*.

> And many of them that sleep in the dust of the earth shall awake, some to everlasting life, and some to shame and everlasting contempt. (Daniel 12:2)

The reason that this week stands out is because it covers the time of creation to the last day. Seven is the number of completeness or fullness in the Bible.

> And all that dwell upon the earth shall worship him, whose names are not written in the book of life of the Lamb slain from the foundation of the world. (Revelation 13:8)

> The beast that thou sawest was, and is not; and shall ascend out of the bottomless pit, and go into

> perdition: and they that dwell on the earth shall wonder, whose names were not written in the book of life from the foundation of the world, when they behold the beast that was, and is not, and yet is. (Revelation 17:8)
>
> According as he hath chosen us in him before the foundation of the world, that we should be holy and without blame before him in love. (Ephesians 1:4)

In Revelation 13:8 and 17:8, we are shown that the names of the elect were written in the Lamb's Book of Life before the foundation of the world. Ephesians 1:4 confirms this by stating that the elect were chosen in Christ from before the foundation of the world.

Next we are told that "and in the midst of the week he shall cause the sacrifice and the oblation to cease." When Christ went to the cross, it not only was the end for animal and temple sacrifices and offerings but became a dividing line. Christ fulfilled the law, and all the sacrifices which were contained in the law were looking forward to Christ and his sacrifice. Therefore, once his sacrifice was completed, animal sacrifices were no longer valid or accepted by God. The year 33 AD was the dividing line in time, and Christ's sacrifice was the dividing line between old and new covenants between law and grace.

> Then said he, Lo, I come to do thy will, O God. he taketh away the first, that he may establish the second. (Hebrews 10:9)

In Hebrews 10:9, we are told that Christ came to take away the first covenant and establish the second covenant. No longer would animal sacrifices ever make a covering for sin. Christ was the final sacrifice for sins, and those who are born again in him never have to worry about making sacrifices or celebrating feasts again. The covenant of grace is without works. Christ going to the cross brought in the period of the New Testament while removing the period of the Old Testament. The midst of the final week represented that dividing line of covenants.

> And for the overspreading of abominations he shall make it desolate, even until the consummation, and that determined shall be poured upon the desolate. (Daniel 9:27)

Even after the crucifixion of Christ, the Jews remained in rank apostasy and were persecuting the followers of Christ. The year 70 AD brought in the determined end of God's patience, and he finally destroyed them fully until the nation of Judah was nothing but a desert place. This just didn't happen but was planned by God, because now that the covenant of grace is fully engaged in the world, he is no longer dealing with only one country but all the countries of the world.

Now when we look at the fact that in the middle of the week Christ was crucified, it means that the rest of the week which is comprised of three and one half days is now representing the entire New Testament period. That term "three and one half" is symbolic as we will see in the following verses:

> But the court which is without the temple leave out, and measure it not; for it is given unto the Gentiles: and the holy city shall they tread under foot forty and two months. (Revelation 11:2)

> And there was given unto him a mouth speaking great things and blasphemies; and power was given unto him to continue forty and two months. (Revelation 13:5)

If you notice in Revelation 11:2 and 5, we have two time periods which are the same, and that is forty-two months, which in the

Jewish calendar is three and a half years, because Jewish months are all thirty days, making the year 360 days.

> 3 And I will give power unto my two witnesses, and they shall prophesy a thousand two hundred and threescore days, clothed in sackcloth. 4 These are the two olive trees, and the two candlesticks standing before the God of the earth. (Revelation 11:3–4)

Let us look at Revelation 11:3–4 where it speaks about the two witnesses which will prophesy or declare the gospel for a period of 1,260 days. If we divide 1,260 by 30, we come out with 42 months. So we see that the two witnesses will preach for three and one-half years. If that number was literal, then we would be in trouble, because when would that period begin and end? The two witnesses are the church of God who will take the gospel to the ends of the earth in the New Testament period.

After Messiah was cut off in the midst of the week, we know that is referring to the crucifixion of Christ; then those days following which are represented by the three and one half days would be the entire New Testament period ending on the last day.

> 1 God, who at sundry times and in divers manners spake in time past unto the fathers by the prophets, 2 Hath in these last days spoken unto us by his Son, whom he hath appointed heir of all things, by whom also he made the worlds. (Hebrews 1:1–2)

Notice in Hebrews 1:1–2, we are told that we are to listen to the Lord Jesus Christ "in these last days." The last days commenced at the cross and will end on the last day of recorded history. Just one more confirmation in this section. Revelation 11:4 states the two witnesses are also known as the "two candlesticks." When we look at Revelation 1:20, it confirms that what is in view is the church, because it calls the church "the two candlesticks."

> The mystery of the seven stars which thou sawest in my right hand, and the seven golden candlesticks. The seven stars are the angels of the seven churches: and the seven candlesticks which thou sawest are the seven churches. (Revelation 1:20)

When it speaks about the church, it is not speaking about local churches or denominations but the true believers which are the real church that are within all the local churches. Churches have both believers and unbelievers in them, and this is true for all churches in the world. I have never come across a local church with all saved people in them.

To summarize this section, what is believed by many to be a literal three and a half year tribulation period is really symbolic for the whole New Testament period, which we saw so plainly by just comparing Scripture with Scripture, which is God's method of understanding the Bible that he gave to us. Prophecy has been made so complex, simply because comparing Scripture with Scripture is ignored.

Judgment Day

The most dreaded day, which the human race is going to face someday, will be Judgement Day. It is the time when all the unbelievers will stand before the Lord Jesus Christ and give an account of their lives to him. All those who appear before his judgment seat will be judged for their sins, and then the ultimate sentence will be given to them, and that will be eternal damnation in hell. There is a popular and erroneous teaching which has permeated the churches that the believers are going to be raised in the rapture before the mythical tribulation period, which we previously studied, and then all the unbelievers will be raised after the mythical millennium. This means there is a period of 1,007 years between resurrections. This is nowhere taught in the Bible, because this belief is another man-made invention.

> 28 Marvel not at this: for the hour is coming, in the which all that are in the graves shall hear his voice, 29 And shall come forth; they that have done good, unto the resurrection of life; and they that have done evil, unto the resurrection of damnation. (John 5:28–29)

If you notice in John 5:28–29, we read "all that are in the graves," which means that every grave in the world will be opened and all those who are in them, whether believer or unbeliever, will be resurrected and come forth. We see two sets of people in these verses, and that is we see the believers, "they that have done good;" and then we see the unbelievers, "they that have done evil." Both of these groups will be raised in one general resurrection at one time.

> 31 When the Son of man shall come in his glory, and all the holy angels with him, then shall he sit upon the throne of his glory: 32 And before him shall be gathered all nations: and he shall separate them one from another, as a shepherd divideth his sheep from the goats: 33 And he shall set the sheep on his right hand, but the goats on the left. 34 Then shall the King say unto them on his right hand, Come, ye blessed of my Father, inherit the kingdom prepared for you from the foundation of the world: (Matthew 25:31–34)

In Matthew 25:31–34, we read a very detailed description as to what will happen right after that general resurrection. There is going to be a separation right at the Judgment Seat of Christ. Christ will set the sheep on his right, which are the true believers who were redeemed by him at Calvary. Then secondly, he will place the goats on the left which are the unbelievers. The believers will go right into the kingdom of heaven, and the unbelievers will go to Judgment.

> Then shall he say also unto them on the left hand, Depart from me, ye cursed, into everlasting fire, prepared for the devil and his angels. (Matthew 25:41)

These verses are very clear that there is going to be one general resurrection. If there was a 1,007 years between resurrections, then how is it possible that the unbelievers are standing with the believers before the final separation? The separation should then take place by means of the 1,007-year span between them, but as we saw, the Bible does not teach separate resurrections but only one general resurrection at one specific time.

Prophecy Books

One of the most needless collection of Christian books are those called "prophecy books," which are written by prophecy preachers and teachers who believe they can predict the future of this world and all the events leading up to it. Prophecy books are not based upon the Bible but are based upon conjecture, news reports, magazines, newspapers, and internet websites by self-proclaimed prophecy preachers who think they can predict world events. These prophecy moguls have butchered the meanings of Scripture and have caused many Christians to walk around in a state of paranoia. When I was a young Christian in 1980–81, I began my Christian walk listening to Jack Van Impe and his prophecy ministry. I sent for materials and heard all about:

- The 10-Nation Common Market.
- The physical Antichrist.
- The mark of the beast.
- 666.
- The invasion of Israel by Russia.

- The physical persecution of the Christians.
- The restoration of the Jews.
- Two-thirds of all Jews being killed.
- Armageddon in the Plains of Megiddo.
- The 1,000-year reign of Christ.
- Seven-year tribulation period.
- The judgment of the believers.
- Pre-Trib rapture.
- Dispensationalism.
- The Rebuilding of the temple.
- Animal Sacrifices reinstated in the temple.

The above sixteen points represent the standard beliefs of those who have adopted the pre-millennial teaching. Prophecy books are written as Hollywood-style sensationalism. If they weren't, they would not sell. Each prophecy mogul writes these books to appeal to the desire Christians have for the thrill of world events. The reality is these prophecy books make up scenarios that never come to pass, and when the prophecy writers are proven wrong, they do not apologize; instead, they just write another one.

If one goes into a Christian bookstore, they will see shelves full of these volumes of lies, but because they read like a Chuck Norris action movie script, people buy them. I know, I fell into that trap as a new Christian. My admonition is that you do not purchase any of these prophecy books, because they will lead you totally astray from solid biblical understanding.

One of the big teachings of these prophecy preachers is that Russia is supposed to invade Israel, according to their understanding of Ezekiel 38:2. Here is how easy it is to debunk these Hollywood movie scripts of theirs.

> Son of man, set thy face against Gog, the land of Magog, the *chief prince* of Meshech and Tubal, and prophesy against him. (Ezekiel 38:2)

This is an absolute butchering of Scripture. The words "chief prince" in this verse is the Hebrew word *rosh*, and guess how the prophecy moguls interpret it? You got it—Russia! The word *rosh* means "head or chief, whether in place, rank or time, or an individual head." Tell me, what does that have to do with Russia? And how do you get Russia out of a word that simply means "chief?" The word is used ninety-seven times in the Old Testament, all translated with a meaning of "chief or head." So why does Ezekiel 38:2 mean Russia and the other ninety-six something different?

This is just one aspect of these preachers of sensationalism. We have already debunked some of their other teachings previously in this book, and we saw how the Bible and their prophecies are at odds with each other. Avoid these types of books at all costs. Don't waste your money on something based on newspapers or other news sources instead of the Bible.

The Book of Revelation

Just a quick note on the Book of Revelation. The pre-millennialists see the book as a chronological book which is another false belief based on their prophecy books. The Book of Revelation is not a chronological book, and here is why. It is broken down into seven visions beyond Chapters 1–3 which were messages to the seven churches.

John's first vision was Chapters 4–7: We read that the judgments affect one-fourth of the earth.

The second parallel vision is Chapters 8–11: There we read about one third of the earth being affected. This means that the second vision is parallel to the first, but it's showing an intensifying of the judgments.

The third parallel vision is Chapters 12–14: Ends in the reaping of the earth.

The fourth vision is Chapters 15–16, which contains the vial judgments which affect the whole earth (one-fourth to one-third to the whole earth) and ends with Armageddon which is the final battle between Christ and Satan.

The fifth vision is Chapters 17–18, which is the destruction of the kingdom of Satan.

The sixth vision is Chapters 19–20, which details the second coming of the Lord Jesus Christ and the final judgment of the unsaved.

The seventh vision is Chapters 21–22, which is the New Heaven and the New Earth.

The reason that you can tell these are based upon separate visions is because if it was a chronological book, then the return of the Lord Jesus Christ should be listed only once in this book; instead, it is listed four times in the following Scriptures:

Revelation 6:12–17
Revelation 11:18–19
Revelation 14:14–16
Revelation 19

The book of Revelation ends with the new heavens and the new earth being created by God. The old heaven and earth will be burned up and all the sin with it, plus the believers will dwell in the new heavens and new earth where righteousness dwell for eternity.

> Nevertheless we, according to his promise, look for new heavens and a new earth, wherein dwelleth righteousness. (2 Peter 3:13)

The Cold Water Principle

> He that receiveth a prophet in the name of a prophet shall receive a prophet's reward; and he that receiveth a righteous man in the name of a righteous man shall receive a righteous man's reward. {42} And whosoever shall give to drink unto one of these little ones a cup of cold water only in the name of a disciple, verily I say unto you, he shall in no wise lose his reward.
> —Matthew 10:41–42)

Here, Jesus speaks of receiving those who are involved in the ministry. Jesus is saying that he that receives a prophet, in the name of a prophet, shares in his reward. This may be the type of prophet which is not necessarily foretelling future events but one who declares the word of God. If one receives them and gives them hospitality, then those people who help the preacher in his ministry are sharing in his ministry. This is why there is no such thing as a small part in ministry.

Let us say you have a visiting preacher coming to your church for a series of meetings. You are asked to design a flyer to hand out; in essence, you are receiving that preacher and will share in his ministry. A word to wives. Let us say that you do all the work around the house, thus freeing your husband to do ministry; you are sharing in his ministry. Then Jesus speaks about receiving a righteous man. Let us say the righteous man is not a preacher but has the gift or ability to build houses or repair them. You may be a helper to this man, but you are sharing in his ministry. You will also share in the rewards of the ministry. What is the greatest reward a Christian can receive?

> After these things the word of the LORD came unto Abram in a vision, saying, Fear not, Abram: I am thy shield, and thy exceeding great reward. (Genesis 15:1)

It is the promise of God himself being our reward. If you are helping a preacher or helping a person do repairs on a church building, it all comes down to one thing, and that is service. You are taking whatever talent or ability the Lord gave you and are using it to the glory of God. So never think that any task is menial in the kingdom of God.

Then in verse 42, Jesus takes it down another notch to just a cup of cold water. He is repeatedly emphasizing that not every single task in the kingdom of God is going to be a large task, and just because a person is doing a task which seems very small, they too will share in the reward. It takes many working together and some doing the bigger tasks and some doing the smaller tasks to bring together a ministry that sends out the Gospel.

Sometimes I hear on the radio ministries which state that you should not hesitate to send in $5 or $10, and that is true, because they add up; and as they add up, they widen the outreach of ministry. So never look at a ministry task as being too small for being useful, because Jesus doesn't, and neither should you.

Back in the 1990s, two television programs premiered which emphasized teamwork. One was *Hercules: The Legendary Journeys*, and the other was *Xena: Warrior Princess*. In the program *Hercules*, he traveled with a companion named Iolaus who shared in all the campaigns of Hercules to help him attain whatever goal he was focusing on in the particular episode. By the way, Kevin Sorbo, who played Hercules, is a born-again Christian.

In the program *Xena*, she travelled with Gabrielle who was her companion in helping her attain whatever goal she was seeking. In both cases, Gabrielle and Iolaus were called sidekicks, which is also a synonym for "associate, partner, or colleague." In other words, they were not secondary or inferior to their partners but played a strategic role in whatever venture they attempted.

These are two good visible examples of how Christianity works. We read in Matthew 10:41–42 that the Lord is talking about a cup of cold water which is probably the most basic thing you can do for someone, but for the someone who is receiving the water and if they are parched, it is a welcome gift. The Lord wants all his children to know that there is no such thing as a meaningless and unnoticed task in Christianity.

> For God is not unrighteous to forget your work and labour of love, which ye have shewed toward his name, in that ye have ministered to the saints, and do minister. (Hebrews 6:10)

The Lord is emphasizing the fact that no matter what your role is in ministry, it is an important one. Remember the person who made the fliers for the visiting preacher. Christianity is a partnership where we partner with other believers for the purpose of getting the Gospel out to the world.

Let's say you do not have the gift of speaking or mercy, or you couldn't hold a tune in a bucket, but you have six extra Bibles at home, so you send them out to a ministry which will forward them to six different indigenous evangelists in the world. Those six Bibles are now being used to preach the gospel in places you never heard of, and people who heard the gospel have become saved. The reality is that those six Bibles were your cup of cold water, and as a result, you shared in the ministry of those itinerant preachers, simply because you sent the six bibles for distribution.

If a thousand people became saved under their preaching from the Bibles you sent, then you have shared in the salvation of those thousand people. The Lord also wants us to know that it does not take much to be a partaker in ministry, but some type of involvement is definitely necessary. Satan could have deceived you by saying that, "Well, what good are six Bibles? It won't have any impact, so you might as well not send them." Can you imagine if you would have believed him? There is a severe shortage of Bibles in the world, and even just six can make an impact for the Lord.

Let's look at another scenario. We have a husband and wife, and the husband is involved in some type of public ministry. Now the husband needs time to prepare sermons, written materials, or whatever his ministry requires. If the wife takes up the mantle of taking care of the home and even the finances, it frees her husband up to continue to do ministry. She shares in the ministry of her husband for two reasons. First, she is one flesh with her husband, and the second is that her function of taking over household duties is her cup of cold water, and she will share in the rewards of her husband's ministry. Now let me interject that this does not mean the husband is to shirk any or all duties around the house and not give his wife a helping hand when he is able to.

There is one fallacy which permeates even Christianity and it is the belief that the person at the forefront of ministry is the one who receives all the credit. Unfortunately, those who minister behind the scenes are normally the forgotten ones; but we should keep in mind the great promise God gives us in Hebrews 6:10 that he will never forget the work we do for the kingdom of God and for the saints when we aid in their ministry, even if it is handing out flyers or even creating them. There are no secondary jobs in the kingdom of God. All have value no matter how small they are.

> And hast made us unto our God kings and priests:
> and we shall reign on the earth. (Revelation 5:10)

In Revelation 5:10, we read that God has made us kings and priests, and we will rule on the earth. It does not say he made "some" kings, but all Christians are kings. This means that Christianity is a faith of equality, no matter what position the Lord puts you in. Whatever position the Lord places you in, just be faithful and fulfill the duties, even if you are overqualified for the job you are doing.

> Moreover it is required in stewards, that a man be
> found faithful. (1 Corinthians 4:2)

Summary

The cold water principle is very simple. You just help get the gospel out in any way you are able to, even if the job you are doing is very humble. If you do not fall into the satanic trap that others will get the credit and you will get nothing, then you will find that your ministry capabilities will be used of the Lord, even if you never walk out on stage or get a trophy.

Remember, we are not home yet! So continue to seek where you can give a cup of cold water and never be hindered by the fact that you are behind the scenes. Always keep in mind the promise of Hebrews 6:10. The only thing God forgets is our sins and iniquities.

> For I will be merciful to their unrighteousness, and their sins and their iniquities will I remember no more. (Hebrews 8:12)

God never forgets our works and labors of love.

What Is a Christian?

As you progress in your Christian walk, you will no doubt hear people claiming themselves to be Christians, so it is important that you know exactly what a Christian is, because the world has many ways of explaining things which are antithetical to the scriptures.

The Name "Christian"

When a person becomes saved, they go from being an unbeliever to a believer. The name Christian is given to the redeemed who follow the Lord Jesus Christ. The name Christian is used three times in the New Testament.

> And when he had found him, he brought him unto Antioch. And it came to pass, that a whole year they assembled themselves with the church, and taught much people. And the disciples were called Christians first in Antioch. (Acts 11:26)
>
> Then Agrippa said unto Paul, Almost thou persuadest me to be a Christian. (Acts 26:28)
>
> Yet if any man suffer as a Christian, let him not be ashamed; but let him glorify God on this behalf. (1 Peter 4:16)

WHAT IS A CHRISTIAN?

It is the Greek word *christianos*. It carries with it the meaning of "followers of Christ." It is believed that the term was first used in Syrian Antioch as far back as 44 AD. The word in the Greek is a proper name and noun. Originally, it was used as a term of derision or ridicule of the followers of Christ, but later, the term was well-accepted. It is like the term *cowboy*, which originally was a term of ridicule in the old west but eventually became an accepted term. The name Christian was also turned into an adjective which describes a noun. It is used in the following manner such as Christian music, Christian books, Christian hospital, etc.

The Substance of a Christian

The world defines a Christian as a person who is not Jewish. They also see a Christian as one who attends church regardless of denomination. Some even believe they are born Christians, because they live in America or some western European country. That is called political Christianity, which has nothing to do with salvation. These are all secular definitions of what they believe a Christian is. Based on these misunderstandings, many, especially those who attend church every week, think they are ready for heaven, and therein lies the great deception. They are only religious sinners, and the fact that they are sinners, religious or not, means they are not true Christians.

There is only one way to become a true Christian, and that is when you are born again in Christ. When you became saved, you went from being an unbeliever to a believer, and that only happens when the Holy Spirit indwells the person in Christ. The only true Christian is a born-again Christian. Outside of being born again, one is not a Christian. That is an irrefutable biblical reality.

How to Identify False Teachers

> But there were false prophets also among the people, even as there shall be false teachers among you, who privily shall bring in damnable heresies, even denying the Lord that bought them, and bring upon themselves swift destruction.
> —2 Peter 2:1

If there is one Bible promise that can define the times we live in, it is false teachings will be rampant. We live in a time when those who cannot rule in a church, because of heresies they possess, can take those same heresies and build a cheap website and propagate those teachings to the entire world without anyone to check them or stop them. One thing that is true is that those who are nothing in their church can set themselves up as something on the internet. This does not mean that false teachings are only found online, but there are still many false teachers, and this includes pastors, theologians, and media ministers on the radio and on the TV. You can also include in that satellite radio.

In other words, there is going to be a large number of false teachers coming into our homes, and if we do not seek to be discerning, then we will fall for the false teachings, which are always palatable. In this chapter, I want to give eighteen warnings to help you avoid falling into the grips of a false teacher. When it comes to false teachers, we are not talking about temporary consequences, but unless a person is following the true Gospel, the consequences will be eternal.

A false gospel is a portal to eternal damnation in a lake of fire in hell for the unsaved. This is why it is so important to discern what you are listening to and what you accept as truth. Agreeing with the crowd does not necessarily mean you are following the right teachings. I do hope these eighteen warnings will help you discern as to whether you are in a true or false church or under the teachings of a true or false teacher.

Men Pleasers

"For do I now persuade men, or God? or do I seek to please men? for if I yet pleased men, I should not be the servant of Christ" (Galatians 1:10).

If there is one major characteristic of a false teacher, it is that they are men pleasers. In Galatians 1:10, the word *pleased* carries with it the meaning of "accommodate or seeking to please." Basically, they are spiritual chameleons, and what I mean by that is it depends on who they are speaking with or what group they are addressing. They will tailor their message to be acceptable while they inject their own beliefs or false teachings. They seek to be crowd pleasers so they can easily win the hearts of their hearers.

Only They Have the Truth

Another characteristic of false teachers is that they claim they are the only ones who possess the truth. They claim that God has given them specific understanding of certain passages and that all the interpretations down through history have been wrong. They rely on the misuse and misunderstanding of progressive revelation.

Progressive revelation is when God gives information on a subject in the Scriptures, and then in a later book of the Bible, he builds on that truth with more information. What the false teacher does is claim that God has giving them understanding outside of the parameters of the Bible. Be very aware of those who claim to have new revelation! God has given millions of copies of the true Scriptures for his children, which means that those who possess a Bible also possess the truth, so it is not limited to any one person.

They Contradict the Truth of Scripture

"Within two full years will I bring again into this place all the vessels of the LORD'S house, that Nebuchadnezzar king of Babylon took away from this place, and carried them to Babylon" (Jeremiah 28:3).

In Jeremiah 28, a false prophet named Hananiah had contradicted the prophesy of Jeremiah. Jeremiah had prophesied that Judah would go into captivity with the Babylonians for a full seventy years, yet this false prophet was telling the people that their captivity will last only a period of two years. For his false prophecies, Hananiah incurred the wrath of God and died that same year.

> So Hananiah the prophet died the same year in the seventh month. (Jeremiah 28:17)

You will eventually hear a charismatic claim that physical healing was part of the atonement. There is no such thing in Scripture, yet they continue to teach such lies. If physical healing was part of the atonement, then why are there church cemeteries? And why do Christians die? False teachers will teach annihilation instead of eternal damnation.

> And whosoever was not found written in the book of life was cast into the lake of fire. (Revelation 20:15)

False teachers will teach it is possible to reach God without Christ.

> Jesus saith unto him, I am the way, the truth, and the life: no man cometh unto the Father, but by me. (John 14:6)

There are many more contradictions to Scripture which are being presented by false teachers today.

HOW TO IDENTIFY FALSE TEACHERS

They Rely on Personal Experience Such as Dreams, Visions or False Prophecies

Until the time the Bible was completed, God did use dreams, visions, and prophecies to reach his people at various times in history. When the Bible was completed, we now have the full word of God, and no longer is the Word of God fragmented, a little here and a little there. With the completion of the Bible, the method of dreams, visions, and prophecies had come to an end. Whenever we need to search something out, we do not seek a dream, vision, or a sign, but we go to the word of God.

False teachers continue to rely on dreams, visions, and prophecies to further their ministry. You will hear false teachers on TV say something like this: "God told me..." Benny Hinn stated that the Lord told him to tell us that he was going to destroy all homosexuals by 1994–95. Guess what? They are still here. Joseph Smith of the Mormons made a prophecy in 1835 that the end of the world would come in fifty-six years, which would make it 1891. He claims this information was given by vision and by the Holy Spirit. Guess what? It didn't happen!

In 1847, Ellen White of the Seventh Day Adventists had a vision that she was taken to the Holy City and came upon the tablets of the Ten Commandments which were in the Ark of the Covenant that Jesus opened for her. She saw a halo of glory surrounding the Fourth Commandment, and thus was the beginning of the Seventh Day Adventists all based on a vision. Beware of those who still claim visions, prophecies, and dreams!

They Decry Certain Teachings of Scripture Like Hell or Sin

False teachers will never teach anything which could cause their audiences to reject them. They will stay away from the doctrines which will make them feel uncomfortable such as sin, hell, or judgment. Joel Osteen has one of the largest churches in the country that does not teach on hell or sin. If he did, he would not be able to keep up his lavish lifestyle. He states that he wants to leave those in the hands of God and that he would rather not judge.

> But I will forewarn you whom ye shall fear: Fear him, which after he hath killed hath power to cast into hell; yea, I say unto you, Fear him. (Luke 12:5)

If Jesus taught it, then it must be taught. False teachers omit anything which might come between them and their donations.

They Focus Heavily on the Love of God

False teachers focus heavily on the love of God, simply because it is a palatable teaching, and the false teacher can easily claim that like God, they too love everyone, which is a draw to lonely or outcast people who are hearing them. However, the Scriptures teach something totally opposite, that God's love is totally qualified and that he does not love the sinner.

> The foolish shall not stand in thy sight: thou hatest all workers of iniquity. (Psalm 5:5)

The word *hatest* in this verse carries with it the meaning of "foe, enemy, odious, and to hate." They focus on the love of God while ignoring some of the other attributes of God such as Judge or Holiness. The false teachers use a tactic called "love bombing," which makes them sound like everything they are doing is sourced only in love. This is how cults recruit new members. It is a tactic which never goes out of date. Remember, love cannot drown out truth!

They Focus a Lot on Material Things Like Money or Houses

Four of the most dangerous TV networks are TBN (Trinity Broadcasting Network), Daystar, Impact, and Inspiration Network.

These four networks continually broadcast the false prosperity and healing preachers, and you must be very discerning when listening. Many of the false charismatic preachers aired are multimillionaires living in mansions and riding around in Bentleys and own private jets. This is just a partial list, because there are probably other networks who air these frauds on other mediums such as radio or Internet.

The main message from these fraudulent preachers are always about money and prosperity. The sorry truth is that the benighted followers of these false teachers are not the ones who are prospering, but only those who are teaching prosperity. Many of them take million-dollar salaries from their ministries.

If you are a donor to one of these false teachers, ask yourself these questions. Why is he or she driving around in a Bentley or a Mercedes, and you are driving around in an old clunker? Why are they living in a mansion, and you are living in a small apartment? Could it be because you are so enthralled by their teachings that you swallowed their lies, without even checking them out once in the Bible? Any preacher that focuses mainly on money is not a preacher of the true Gospel but is a self-serving fraud. A true preacher focuses on the true Gospel and the salvation of souls.

They Manipulate Scripture to Make It Say What They Want

"Vow, and pay unto the LORD your God: let all that be round about him bring presents unto him that ought to be feared" (Psalm 76:11).

Many of us remember some years ago the manipulations of Robert Tilton who built a multimillion-dollar ministry on one simple word: *vow*. He would keep twisting that term until the only thing it meant was to send a $1,000-vow to God; of course, it would go through Tilton. He amassed millions of dollars by twisting this one word of Scripture. One must be very careful if they are listening to a teacher who has such a narrow focus on only one term or subject.

Another manipulation by false teachers is the subject of healing. They teach that God wants everyone healed because it is part of the atonement of Christ. Yet, charismatic churches all have cemeteries. Why would they need them if physical healing was part of the atonement?

They Normally Come from Inside the Church

"Also of your own selves shall men arise, speaking perverse things, to draw away disciples after them" *(Acts 20:30)*.

The Apostle Paul warned the church at Ephesus that false teachers will arise from among the flock and not from the outside. Joseph Smith, the founder of Mormonism, came out of the Methodist Church. Charles Taze Russell, founder of the Jehovah's Witnesses, came out of Presbyterianism and Congregationalism. William Miller, the founder of the Seventh Day Adventists, came out of the Baptist Church.

These are just three examples of false teachers who arose from among Christian congregations. Whenever a pastor or anyone in the congregation hears someone spouting false teachings, they need to be dealt with immediately. So when someone is preaching that God told them to leave their church and start a movement, then you know there is fraud involved, and they need to be vetted thoroughly so others can be warned.

What Type of Living does the Message Teach?

With every type of teaching, there will always come a resulting lifestyle. The Bible speaks about us living a humble existence here on earth.

> And having food and raiment let us be therewith content. *(1 Timothy 6:8)*

What type of living does the false teacher advocate? Is it one of wealth, looking to live in a mansion and have many material goods? Is it one of total abstract poverty where you have absolutely nothing? One can look at the teacher to see what kind of lifestyle they advocate.

What Promises Do They Make to You, Such as Seventy-Two Virgins or God of Your Own Planet?

The Jehovah's Witnesses are always making promises to their people that they will live in paradise on this earth. They have many accompanying artists drawing these scenarios of people living in total bliss. The Muslim men are told they will have seventy-two virgins if they die in a jihad against infidels. The Mormons are promised they will be gods of their own planet. The eastern religions, like Hinduism and Buddhism, promise nirvana. The prosperity preachers always state that if you seed some money—of course, to their ministry—then God is going to prosper you with much wealth, and then they teach about men like Abraham or Job who had much material goods. What about Peter Popoff guaranteeing you a miracle if you send for his miracle spring water? It is very important to listen to what promises they make you and see if they line up with Scripture.

False Teachers Will Never Accept Correction

False teachers will always do the correcting since they believe that God has chosen them to be his voice in this world. I remember when the late Harold Camping of Family Radio was predicting the end of the world on May 21, 2011. Many godly men went to him and counseled him to stop going further in these predictions and to stop attacking the church as Camping claimed that all pastors and theologians were under the judgment of God and were hell-bound if they didn't leave the church.

Of course, Camping would not take any correction or even consider the things these godly men were saying. It is something that I am writing this section in May 2019, eight years after the supposed return of Christ. We are still here because no one can ever know the day or hour of Christ's return. So if you encounter someone teaching falsely and will not take any correction, run for your life from them. These people are always correct in their own eyes, and everyone else is wrong.

False Teachers Always Appeal to the Flesh

False teachers will always appeal to the flesh. That is, they always focus on the here and now and never give concern about the future. They teach health and wealth but never broach the more serious subjects of eternity. They do not care if their hearers go to hell as long as they get their false message across and accepted. If their message is slanted only toward the present, without concern for your soul, then leave them and do not look back.

They Draw People unto Themselves and Not God

"Also of your own selves shall men arise, speaking perverse things, to draw away disciples after them" (Acts 20:30).

They claim to be speaking for God, but the reality is that they are drawing away disciples after themselves. They look to be front and center and the center focus of the spiritual life of their disciples. These can be seen in strong central figures like David Koresh, Jim Jones, and Sun Myung Moon. All three of these came out of the church.

The Apostle John also faced the problem of someone as a strong central figure.

> I wrote unto the church: but Diotrephes, who loveth to have the preeminence among them, receiveth us not. *(3 John 9)*

Apparently, Diotrephes was one of these church bosses who wanted to be the central figure in the church. This type of person is one who has an overbearing personality and will not be challenged.

They Turn You Away from the Teachings of the Bible with Sources Like Mysticism, Especially in the Emergent Church Movement

In our day, there is a great turning away from the Bible, and in place of Bible study, there is an emphasis upon experience. This can be seen in something called "The Emergent Church Movement." In this movement, Bible study is frowned upon while experience is encouraged. They encourage studies in the areas of Roman Catholic Mysticism. They believe in clearing the mind and allowing soaking prayer which is:

> Soaking prayer is one such mystical activity. It is described as resting in God's presence. This is accomplished by playing some gentle worship songs, either sitting or lying down, and praying short, simple prayers for an extended period of time, but otherwise keeping your mind free of other thoughts. At the point when you sense God's presence through some type of manifestation like tingling skin, a sensation of heat or cold, or even a gentle wind seemingly blowing through your body, you are to just "soak" in that presence.[4]

The poison seeping into the church is called "Christian Mysticism," which states that there is no need for Bibles or even verbal praying. They use a form of mind-clearing techniques which open the door for demonic suggestion. It is called the "Apophatic Method" whereby a person completely empties their mind and then tries to become one with God.

These methods are couched in what is called "The Emergent Church Movement," which is dominated by the teachings of Roman Catholic Mystics such as Teresa of Avila (who hated Protestants), John of the Cross, Thomas Merton, Catherine of Sienna, etc. They have levitated in front of people and have had dreams and visions and so-called revelations. Did you know that many Protestant preachers are endorsing this type of evil such as Tony Campolo, Leighton Ford, formerly of the Billy Graham Association, Leonard Sweet, Brian Maclaren, and many others who are falling prey to it?

---

[4] From: http://www.gotquestions.org/soaking–prayer.html

Any teacher that frowns upon the study of the Scriptures and puts experience in its place is a false teacher and must be exposed and rejected.

They Tell You What You Want to Hear

If there is another major principle of our day, it is the principle of palatable teachings. False teachers will always tell you what you want to hear. They will tell you that God loves you and wants you wealthy and well. They will tell you things which appease you and that can in no way be refuted because they are considered good guys.

People want to hear things like universal salvation or that their dog went to heaven. Animal salvation was taught by Jack Van Impe who believed all pets went to heaven, although this is nowhere taught in Scripture. With the way people glorify their pets today, this is one way to tell people what they want to hear and gain donations. False teachers will tell you that good works will get people into heaven when this is nowhere taught in Scripture. It makes people feel good, especially those in false religions like Roman Catholicism, which is a works-based religion.

They Entice People with Great Words

"For when they speak great swelling words of vanity, they allure through the lusts of the flesh, through much wantonness, those that were clean escaped from them who live in error" (2 Peter 2:18).

The word *swelling* in the Greek carries with it the meaning of "excessive, bombastic, or insolent." Their words are nothing but great promises which can never be fulfilled. As the Scripture states, their words are vain and are useless. They will write books or they will write great articles with only some type of positive reinforcement without any reality placed within.

Sometimes, the great swelling words can be found within Christian psychology or even among motivational speakers. Have you ever been conned into multilevel marketing when the one presenting it to you tries to make it a spiritual experience? Do they not use great swelling words to try and con you into signing on for financial freedom? What about those Christian motivational speakers who want to get you to their Bible conferences when, in essence, they are nothing but centers for false teaching? Beware of anyone selling a message which only has positive points but never has any negative or points of reality.

False Teachers May Possess a Messiah Complex

David Koresh believed that he was a messianic figure carrying out a divine mandate. Sun Myung Moon believed he was chosen by God to finish the work of Jesus Christ. Teachers who are placed in areas of prominence by their followers allow their pride to take over, and they tend to believe they are messiahs. This is why preacher worship is not only dangerous to the follower, but also to the preacher himself who starts believing all the messianic words surrounding him.

Within the church are preachers who have almost the same standing as messiahs, whose congregations revere them to the point of near worship.

Summary

I have given eighteen warning signs that a person might be a false teacher. Not every sign will be evident in every false teacher, but at least one of these will be, and they should be listened to several times and compared to the Scriptures to see if they harmonize. Your greatest line of defense against false doctrines and teachers is your King James Bible. The modern versions line up with the Jehovah's Witnesses Bible and the Roman Catholic Bibles, so they will not be much help in exposing false teachers.

Whenever you encounter a false teacher, turn off the radio or just get up and leave if they are live. False teachers represent the kingdom of Satan and are coming after Christians to try and derail them. False teachers must not be given the opportunity to accomplish that.

How to Identify True Teachers

> Am I therefore become your enemy,
> because I tell you the truth?
>
> —Galatians 4:16

Just as there are false teachers with certain characteristics which are very noticeable, there are also true teachers who have some characteristics that are very noticeable. It is not only important that we identify and reject the false teachers who attempt to turn us away from Christ, but it is just as important for us to recognize the true teachers who try to point us to Christ and to live a true Christian life. All one has to do is turn on the radio or TV, and it will be obvious by seeing and listening whether we are in the presence of a true or false teacher. In this chapter, I want to give thirteen characteristics of true teachers. In this way, we can make a proper decision as to what group we are listening to, the false or the true.

They Tell You What You Need to Hear

"And the king of Israel said unto Jehoshaphat, There is yet one man, Micaiah the son of Imlah, by whom we may inquire of the LORD: but I hate him; for he doth not prophesy good concerning me, but evil. And Jehoshaphat said, Let not the king say so" (1 Kings 22:8).

Here is probably a little known prophet of God who lived in the time of King Ahab of the Northern Kingdom of Israel. Ahab hated him because Micaiah would only speak the truth and told Ahab what he needed to hear, not what he wanted to hear.

It is the same with us. Even as Christians, we may adopt a certain lifestyle which may be against Scripture, and when we hear someone challenge our lifestyle, we too may hate the one who is preaching, simply because they are telling the truth. They are speaking what we need to hear and not what we want to hear.

The true teacher will teach the word of God without apology, not concerning themselves with whose toes they are stepping on. The true teacher also teaches the Bible unapologetically to unbelievers, because they know that a person is saved through hearing the word of God and not a bunch of commentary or excuses for the Bible being so straightforward.

Their Message Always Aligns with Scripture

"And a certain Jew named Apollos, born at Alexandria, an eloquent man, and mighty in the scriptures, came to Ephesus" (Acts 18:24). "For he mightily convinced the Jews, and that publicly, shewing by the scriptures that Jesus was Christ" (Acts 18:28).

Here was a man named Apollos who taught the Jews that Jesus was the Christ. In the above passage, we read that he did it not of philosophy or out of some other type of arguments, but he used the Scriptures to convince the Jews that Jesus was the Christ. The message of Apollos had aligned completely with Scripture. The true teacher does not teach from commentaries or from opinion, but they teach directly from the Word of God, which only has the power to convict a person or to convert them to Christianity.

The true teacher does not teach the so-called "gray areas" but sticks completely to black and white; this way, they know they are teaching God's words rather than a mixture of God's word and man's ideas.

They Teach the Full Counsel of God

"For I have not shunned to declare unto you all the counsel of God" (Acts 20:27).

Here we have the Apostle Paul stating that he taught them the full counsel of God. The word *shunned* in the Greek carries with it the meaning of "cower or to shrink back." In other words, there was a boldness in Paul to preach the entire counsel of God which not only included the promises of God, but also the wrath and judgment by God on the last day.

The whole counsel of God includes judgment as well as all the promises. Today, we have a so-called positive message which only focuses on the love of God and what he can do for us. The pulpits today have been very silent in declaring that a judgment day will come to pass, and that is because they want only to appease their hearers, thus increasing donations. Can it be a positive message when only half the story is told, and unbelievers are made to feel good until they stand before the Lord on Judgment Day and be sentenced to hell? The true teacher focuses on the whole message from the Bible and does not intentionally omit any part of it.

They Do Not Seek to Please Men

"For do I now persuade men, or God? or do I seek to please men? for if I yet pleased men, I should not be the servant of Christ" (Galatians 1:10).

The true teacher does not concern themselves with pleasing people with some glossed over stories. They will teach the hard truths of Scripture as well as the pleasant truths of Scripture, such as a guarantee of heaven for every true believer. The true teacher does not customize their message to accommodate those in the audience that may be living in sin or partaking of sins.

For example, if there is a church which has drinkers or smokers, the true teacher will not tailor the message to excuse their sins. They will teach the parts of Scripture which condemn the drinking of alcohol by believers and the bad habit of smoking which leads to death.

>Thou shalt not kill. (Exodus 20:13)

Smoking kills the body and is a lousy testimony. Can you have a Marlboro in one hand and a Bible in another and convince people you have been changed by your salvation? The true teacher expounds the truths of Scripture, no matter who is in the audience.

Their Message Is Based on Scripture and Not Personal Experiences

"For such are false apostles, deceitful workers, transforming themselves into the apostles of Christ" (2 Corinthians 11:13).

The true teacher confines their messages to the Scriptures. Today, you have many who have visions, dreams, and other signs and wonders who base their message upon these personal experiences. The reality is that God is no longer speaking in visions and dreams, because we now have the completed Bible. People have dreams, and right away, they think it is a message from God, when in essence, the dream is in response to what they ate before going to bed.

The true teacher bases all their messages and beliefs upon what the Scriptures teach and not some personal experience which may come right from the pit of hell. They also do not focus on commentaries or the opinions of theologians as irrefutable truth. Rather, they deem the Scriptures as the highest authority, and as a result, they build a lasting stability into their Christian life.

They Focus on the Spiritual Aspect of Your Life

"For the kingdom of God is not meat and drink; but righteousness, and peace, and joy in the Holy Ghost" (Romans 14:17).

If you turn on the TV today, it will not take you long to come across media preachers, and when you listen to them, you will hear that their primary message is all about giving money to God's work and, of course, it is to be given to them. The false teacher claims that if you give them $1,000 in seed money, then God will bless you many times over with wealth and health. They focus on the here and now and the physical and never give thought to the spiritual life of the believer.

The true teacher wants the Christians to have a Godly and closer walk with the Lord. They want to see Christians spiritually progress in their Christian walk, becoming a great witness, and actively involved in personal ministry. They want to see Christians overcome the satanic obstacles in this world and be victorious in their Christian walk.

> He that hath an ear, let him hear what the Spirit saith unto the churches; To him that overcometh will I give to eat of the tree of life, which is in the midst of the paradise of God. (Revelation 2:7)

Notice that Revelation 2:7 states that those who hear what the Spirit says will be those who overcome. It is the spiritual life that we must focus on. Rev. 2:7 nowhere mentions that you can overcome by having much money or material goods. So if you are under the teaching of one who focuses on the spiritual aspect of the Christian walk, then you are under a true teacher.

The Message Is Made Clear

"Let no man deceive you with vain words: for because of these things cometh the wrath of God upon the children of disobedience" (Ephesians 5:6).

The true teacher makes the message of the Bible as clear as possible. They say in 100 words what others may say in 1,000 words. Today the message of the Bible is being clouded with so many different false systems. The latest one to attack the church is the mystical teachings found in the Emergent Church movement which replaces the message of the Bible with all kinds of New Age esoteric mind-control methods which do nothing but engender demonic involvement.

If you are hearing a teacher who is making their comments by way of Scripture, then you have found a true teacher. If you are hearing a teacher who muddies the teaching of Scripture with all kind of vain philosophies and false theologies, then you are under a false teacher. Beware of those who have to overexplain the Bible. The true teacher approaches the Scriptures with the realization that most of the Scriptures are almost self-explanatory. They do not need to overinterpret to the point of actually losing the meaning of a passage. They can normally explain a passage with another passage of Scripture, because spiritual interprets spiritual.

> Which things also we speak, not in the words which man's wisdom teacheth, but which the Holy Ghost teacheth; comparing spiritual things with spiritual. *(1 Corinthians 2:13)*

They Possess Humility When Teaching

"Humble yourselves in the sight of the Lord, and he shall lift you up" (James 4:10).

The true teacher is a humble teacher, because they know that the message is not theirs. They realize that if they humble themselves, then God can easily work with them and open the truths of the Bible to them so they can pass them on to other Christians. They know that there is no place for arrogance in Bible teaching.

This is not to say that a teacher cannot have confidence in the message of the Bible or in delivering truths. The false teacher teaches with an arrogance as if they are delivering a message which cannot be refuted. The true teacher is malleable in the hands of the Lord, which means they can be taught.

They will Accept Correction When Needed

"And he began to speak boldly in the synagogue: whom when Aquila and Priscilla had heard, they took him unto them, and expounded unto him the way of God more perfectly" (Acts 18:26).

Apollos was a teacher of the Gospel, but he had known only the way of John's baptism. So Priscilla and Aquila heard him preach, and afterward, they took him aside and then expounded the word of God to him. In other words, they had given Apollos the true gospel to preach.

Apollos was open for correction and had accepted that correction by two Christians who had now given him the message of the true Gospel.

> Bring Zenas the lawyer and Apollos on their journey diligently, that nothing be wanting unto them. (Titus 3:13)

We can tell that Apollos took the correction because the Apostle Paul had now asked for Apollos. The book of Titus was written about 55 AD. Sometimes, a true teacher will hold a false understanding or a false teaching, but as soon as they find out, then they will change to make their teachings align with the Scriptures.

They Accept Scripture for What It Teaches

"As also in all his epistles, speaking in them of these things; in which are some things hard to be understood, which they that are unlearned and unstable wrest, as they do also the other scriptures, unto their own destruction" (2 Peter 3:16).

The true teacher is one that accepts the teachings of Scripture as taught in the Bible. They do not filter certain verses through their personal bias but instead willingly accept what the Bible plainly teaches. For example:

> Elect according to the foreknowledge of God the Father, through sanctification of the Spirit, unto obedience and sprinkling of the blood of Jesus Christ: Grace unto you, and peace, be multiplied. (1 Peter 1:2)

The first word in this verse is *Elect*. The word *elect* means "chosen or elect." I have heard many freewill preachers explain it away that God looked down the corridors of time and saw who would accept him, and therefore he elected them. My question is why would God have to elect them if they were going to accept him? So you can see how false teachers butcher the simple meaning of *elect*, and this is done with many other words because they are filtered through the bias of a person's belief system or some theological belief system. The true teacher does not seek to change word definitions to suit themselves but teaches them as God has given them in the Bible without apology.

They Are Portals to the Glory of God

"Give unto the LORD the glory due unto his name; worship the LORD in the beauty of holiness" (Psalm 29:2).

A true teacher gives glory to God for the revealing of Bible truths. They know that unless God gives the understanding of the Scriptures, then there would be no true understanding; instead, they would wrest the Scriptures to their own destruction.

The true teacher recognizes that since God wrote the Bible, then he is the only one qualified to interpret it and give the believer the true understanding of Scripture. The false teachers seek to bring glory to themselves as if they are the only ones that have the truth.

> I wrote unto the church: but Diotrephes, who loveth to have the preeminence among them, receiveth us not. (3 John 9)

Here Diotrephes desires to have the preeminence among his congregation. He wished to be glorified as if he was *the* speaker for God in that congregation.

They Realize That They Are Not the Only Ones Who Have the Truth

"Then pleased it the apostles and elders, with the whole church, to send chosen men of their own company to Antioch with Paul and Barnabas; namely, Judas surnamed Barsabas, and Silas, chief men among the brethren" (Acts 15:22).

Here we have two sets of men ready to go out and bring the messages of what was spoken at the Jerusalem conference. Notice that they sent out not only Paul and Barnabas, but also Judas (not Iscariot) and Silas. The true teacher knows that they are not the only ones who hold the truth but are part of a vast network of Christians all over this world who also hold to the truth. In opposition to those false teachers who believe only they have the truth, true teachers are willing to share teaching responsibilities with those of like-mind and who hold the Scriptures higher than man's opinions.

They Do Not Claim Any Promises Outside What the Bible Promises

"And this is the promise that he hath promised us, even eternal life" (1 John 2:25).

The true teacher does not embellish the promises given in Scripture, because they know that they do not have to. If the Scripture states eternal life, then eternal life it is for the true believer. If it is the new heavens and the new earth, then it is to be believed as such.

We hear about Islam promising seventy-two virgins for every man that dies in jihad. We hear that Mormons become gods of their own planets. These things are nowhere found in Scripture, yet these false cults still convince their people they will get these things if they adhere to their rules. The true teacher does not get involved with fanciful interpretations and fantasy beliefs. They stick totally to the Scriptures for their promises.

Summary

I have given thirteen principles how to spot a true teacher. They are sincere and humble and do not cross any unbiblical boundaries. They do not intentionally misquote Scripture but seek to be sincere in their understanding of Scripture so they may pass on these eternal truths to their hearers. You will see that their lifestyle will match their teachings. Their desire is to see Christians progress in their Christian walk. A true teacher is a gem, so value them as they are gifts to your congregation and to you personally.

One of the main ingredients of being a good teacher is the realization that if you are going to present a teaching, it must be researched well, and that will take considerable time. While other Christians are out having a good time, you will have to make the sacrifice of sometimes skipping those outings to study your subject at hand. Those teachers who just grab someone else's material, and then quote it as if they were the one who wrote it, definitely do not have the spiritual gift of teaching.

> He that findeth his life shall lose it: and he that loseth his life for my sake shall find it. (Matthew 10:39)

This is what the Lord speaks about when he says we lose our life in this life. The more time we spend here on earth, researching the Gospel, means that it is less time we have to enjoy the things of this earth. However, there is an upside to this: those who do this will find life on the other side. Teaching is not something which should be entered into lightly since it is a major commitment of time and energy and because you will suffer fatigue; plus, teaching is an ongoing ministry and not just a one-time commitment.

Online Christian Ministries to Help Further Your Growth!

Scion of Zion Internet Ministry—www.scionofzion.com
A Puritan's Mind—www.apuritansmind.com/
Fire and Ice—www.puritansermons.com/
Grace Gems—www.gracegems.org/
Pristine Grace—www.pristinegrace.org/
Protestant Alliance—www.protestant-alliance.org/index.html

Media Ministries

Family Radio—www.familyradio.org/
FBC Radio—www.fbcradio.org/
Bible Broadcasting Network—www.bbnradio.org/
Redeemer Broadcasting—www.redeemerbroadcasting.org
Reign of Grace Media Ministry—www.rofgrace.com/
Word of Grace Ministries—www.wordofgrace.com/
Sermon Audio—www.sermonaudio.com
Mt. Zion Bible Church—www.chapellibrary.org/

Tract Ministries

Chick Publications—www.chick.com/
Moments with the Book—www.mwtb.org

ONLINE CHRISTIAN MINISTRIES TO HELP FURTHER YOUR GROWTH!

Book and Bible Ministries

Cumberland Valley Book Service—www.cvbbs.com/
Reformation Heritage Books—www.heritagebooks.org/
Bearing Precious Seed—www.bpsmilford.org/
Local Church Bible Publishers—www.localchurchbiblepublishers.com/
Church Bible Publishers—www.churchbiblepublishers.com/
The KJV Store—https://www.thekjvstore.com/

King James Bible Ministries

Bible for Today—www.biblefortoday.org
Dean Burgon Society—http://www.deanburgonsociety.org
AV 1611—http://av1611.com/
King James Bible Research Council—http://www.kjbresearchcouncil.com/
Another King James Bible Believer—http://brandplucked.webs.com/
King James Version Clothing Company—https://kjvclothingcompany.com/

Final Thoughts

This book was designed to help you begin your new Christian life on a biblical foundation. If we stray from the Scriptures, we will always get into trouble. I hope you have had a good basic understanding of the subjects we have studied. As older Christians in the faith, it is our responsibility to "feed the lambs" of Christ and do it correctly. This means it is our responsibility to train the next generation. My desire is to train the next generation according to the Scriptures and not church dogma.

> For David, after he had served his own generation by the will of God, fell on sleep, and was laid unto his fathers, and saw corruption: (Acts 13:36)

David served his own generation, and that is the principle which should guide all Christians, no matter how old they are in the faith. We need to seek to reach our generation with the truths of the Bible. Christians need to hunker down and get busy learning the Bible; and it is important that Christians interpret the Bible by the Bible, and not through biased eyes, to teach only what is palatable.

There will be times when you fail in your Christian walk, but don't worry about it. Ask God to forgive you, talk with him about it, and keep your guard up to make sure you don't fall prey to that temptation again. Let me reemphasize that you cannot lose your salvation, even though sometimes we may feel we have.

Never go by feelings; only what God says in the Bible is what counts and what you should believe.

If this book has been helpful to you, then it has achieved its purpose. This book is not only good for new Christians but those who have been in the faith a while, because many times, as we get older in the faith, we forget about those basic tenets we learned as new Christians which, in essence, are the building blocks to our understanding of the scriptures. May God bless you as you begin to follow him!

> And he that sat upon the throne said, Behold,
> I make all things new. And he said unto me, Write:
> for these words are true and faithful. (Revelation 21:5)

About the Author

Ken Matto lives in Whiting, New Jersey. He holds a Doctor of Ministry degree from Bethany Theological Seminary in Dothan, Alabama. His main ministry is on the Internet.

The website, Scion of Zion, has been online for over twenty-one years since November 20, 1997. www.scionofzion.com is viewed in over 150 countries each month.

He has been a Christian since the summer of 1980 when he first ordered materials which focused on prophecy. His interest focused on that subject until he came to the point that many of the verses did not line up with what was being taught. Basically, he saw that many of the verses were being forced to adapt to the teaching at hand.

Over the years, he abandoned these prophecy books and came to the realization that we are to interpret the Bible by the Bible, and not according to prophecy and theology books, and that means all subjects. In line with this, he has noticed from experience that many Christians are biblically illiterate, and he does not say this to denigrate anyone but to point to the fact that many Christians are lacking a good understanding of Scripture, because they were not trained properly as a young Christian in the Scriptures. Dr. Matto wishes to help rectify that situation by offering a book which contains twenty-seven subjects to help a new or young Christian become grounded in the Scriptures.

Once a Christian is grounded in the Scriptures, their growth will be according to the Scriptures and will have greater understanding of the Bible. This will result in stronger Christians who will eventually continue bringing the Gospel to the world in obedience to the Great Commission.

CPSIA information can be obtained
at www.ICGtesting.com
Printed in the USA
FFHW021453230919
55137316-60845FF

9 781098 007294